D0603484

NEPAL
in Pictures

Christine Zuchora-Walske

Twenty-First Century Books

Contents

Twenty-First Century Books
A division of Lerner Publishing Group, Inc.
241 First Avenue North
Minneapolis, MN 55401 U.S.A.

Website address: www.lernerbooks.com

web enhanced @ www.vgsbooks.com

Library of Congress Cataloging-in-Publication Data

Zuchora-Walske, Christine.
    Nepal in pictures / by Christine Zuchora-Walske.
       p.   cm. − (Visual geography series)
    Includes bibliographical references and index.
    ISBN 978-0-8225-8578-7 (lib. bdg. : alk. paper)
       1. Nepal−Juvenile literature. I. Title. II. Series: Visual geography series (Minneapolis, Minn.)
DS493.4.Z83 2009
    954.96−dc22   2007038573

Manufactured in the United States of America
1 2 3 4 5 6 − BP − 14 13 12 11 10 09

INTRODUCTION

Nepal is a land of extreme contrasts in southern Asia. This small nation's geography ranges from tropical lowlands teeming with life to the world's highest mountains, the Himalayas, hostile to all who venture there. Between the extremes lie a rich variety of habitats and a vast array of living species.

Nepal's human landscape is as varied as its natural one. For centuries, the region within Nepal's modern borders included many small kingdoms. These kingdoms mostly followed the ancient religion of Hinduism, which arose in neighboring India. The Shah family unified the kingdoms in the late 1700s. Not long afterward, Nepal became a forbidden realm. From 1846 until 1951, the ruling Rana family allowed only a handful of outsiders into the country—and permitted very few Nepalis to exit. This isolation protected Nepal from colonization while many of its neighbors submitted to European rule. But isolation also hindered the country's economic and social development.

In 1951 an anti-Rana movement placed the Shahs back in power,

ending Nepal's long isolation. Tourists attracted by the Himalayas began flocking to Nepal. They found a beautiful land whose people had a rich and unique mix of cultural, ethnic, and religious traits. Through tourism and other foreign contact, Nepalis learned about advances in the rest of the world. They began the slow process of catching up with modern scientific, political, social, and cultural ideas.

Though Nepal has experienced great change during the past half century, its culture still owes much to ancient influences. Thousands of years ago, Indians moved into Nepal from the south and west, bringing the Hindu religion with them. Tibetans entered the region from the north and east, contributing their animist spirituality. (Animists believe spirits inhabit natural places, beings, things, and the everyday world.) After Siddhartha Gautama (Buddha) was born in Nepal in the sixth century B.C., Buddhism joined the mix.

Throughout most of Nepal's history, its rulers and its people have been very tolerant of diverse cultural influences. As a result, many

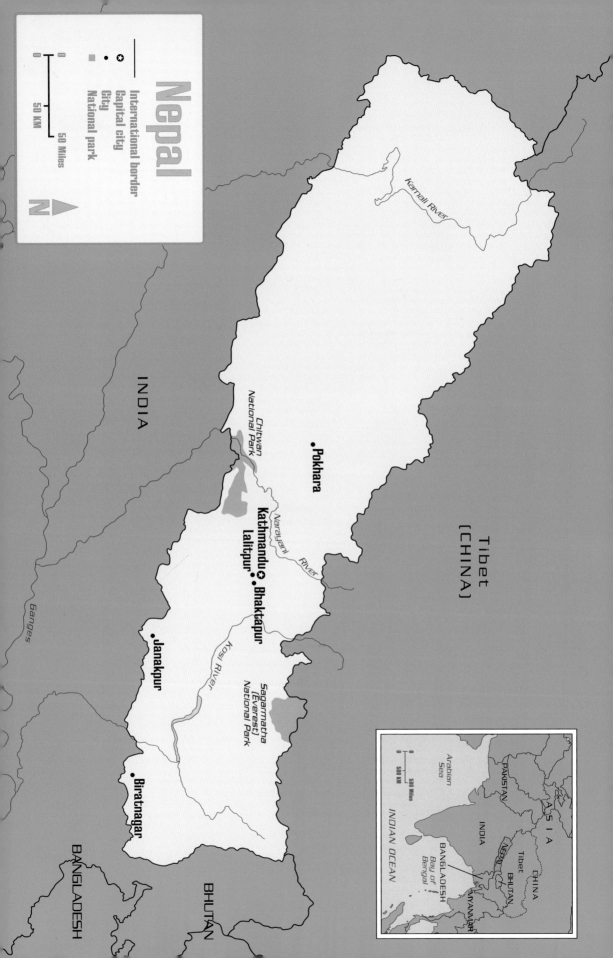

Nepal

- — International border
- ⊛ Capital city
- • City
- ▪ National park

0
0
50 KM
50 Miles

N

Karnali River

INDIA

Chitwan
National Park

• Pokhara

Narayani River

Kathmandu ⊛
Lalitpur • • Bhaktapur

• Janakpur

Kosi River

Sagarmatha
(Everest)
National Park

• Biratnagar

Ganges

BANGLADESH

BHUTAN

Tibet
[CHINA]

PAKISTAN

Arabian
Sea

0
0
500 KM
500 Miles

A S I A

INDIA

CHINA

Tibet

NEPAL

BHUTAN

BANGLADESH

Bay of
Bengal

MYANMAR

INDIAN OCEAN

ethnic groups arose there. Each formed a unique society that molded aspects of Indian and Tibetan cultures to suit its own needs.

Nepal's people are not, however, tolerant of unjust, self-serving, or incompetent rulers. Ever since they threw out the authoritarian Rana government in 1951, Nepalis have been struggling—slowly but steadily—away from monarchy and toward democracy. This journey has seen dozens of governments rise and fall, many political movements born, and thousands of lives lost. The Nepali Civil War (1996–2006) tore the country apart. In 2007 the monarchy finally gave up its power. A temporary government committed to democratic ideals began the work of organizing elections to a new Constituent Assembly. The assembly elected in April 2008 will in turn write a new Nepali constitution.

Nepal is well on its way to a more democratic future. But its new government faces a daunting task. The nation's 27.8 million citizens are among the poorest people in the world. Their leaders must not only heal political wounds but also improve economic and social conditions to create lasting peace and freedom. Because they've come so far already, Nepalis face these new challenges with confidence.

Visit www.vgsbooks.com for links to websites with additional information about Nepal.

THE LAND

Nepalis call their country "a yam between two boulders." Nepal is a small southern Asian nation nestled among the Himalaya mountains between two giant neighbors. India forms Nepal's western, southern, and eastern borders. The region of Tibet (a once-independent nation governed by China) borders Nepal to the north, on the other side of the highest Himalayan peaks. Nepal has an average length of 550 miles (885 kilometers) and an average width of 120 miles (193 km). It covers an area of 56,827 square miles (147,181 sq. km). The country is about the same size as the state of Florida.

◉ Topography

Despite its small size, Nepal is home to a startling range of terrain. Between its southern and northern borders, altitudes climb from 230 feet (70 meters) above sea level to 29,035 feet (8,850 m)—the highest point on Earth. Nepal contains three main regions: the Terai, the Hills, and the Greater Himalaya mountain region.

The Terai runs along Nepal's southern border. It's a sliver of northern India's Ganges Plain. (The Ganges River flows from west to east across northern India.) The Terai is a long, narrow strip of flat, marshy grassland and forest. Because it is Nepal's most level and fertile region, many farms dot the Terai. It provides most of the nation's food.

The Terai makes up about 23 percent of Nepal's land. Its altitude ranges from 230 to 656 feet (70 to 200 m) above sea level. Many rivers that begin in the mountains cross the region. These waterways dump tons of silt, sand, gravel, and boulders there.

The Siwalik Range marks the beginning of Nepal's Hills region. This range makes up the outermost foothills of the Himalayas. The Mahabharat Range to the north parallels the Siwalik Range. The Hills region also includes the Midlands, a highland area with gentle slopes. The Hills make up about 42 percent of Nepal's land. Altitudes in the region range from 656 to 9,843 feet (200 to 3,000 m). Swift rivers have carved deep valleys throughout the Hills.

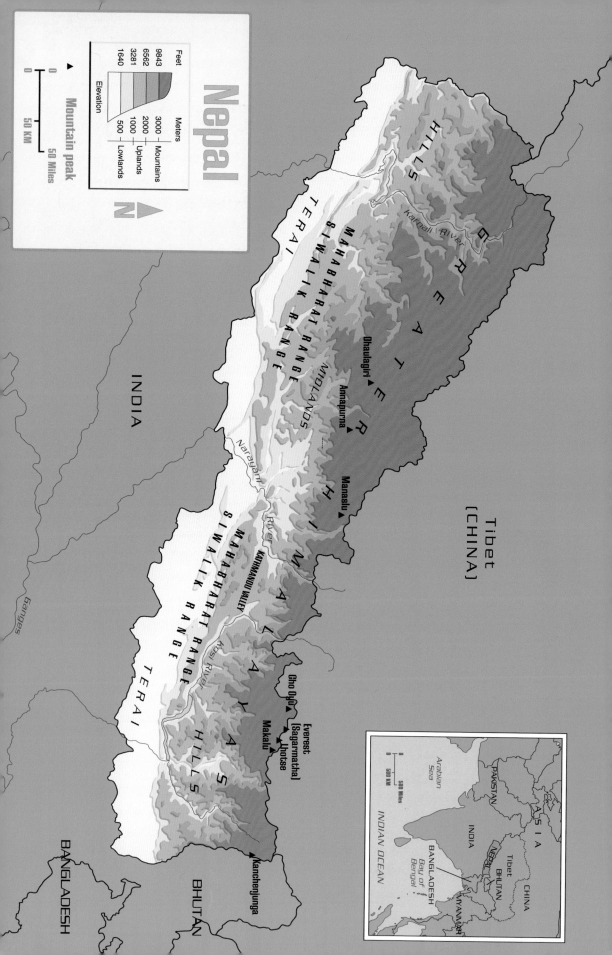

Nepal

Elevation

Feet	Meters	
9843	3000	Mountains
6562	2000	
3281	1000	Uplands
1640	500	Lowlands

▲ Mountain peak

N

0 — 50 KM
0 — 50 Miles

GREATER HIMALAYAS

MIDLANDS

MAHABHARAT RANGE

SIWALIK RANGE

HILLS

TERAI

Karnali River

Narayani River

Kosi River

Dhaulagiri ▲

Annapurna ▲

Manaslu ▲

KATHMANDU VALLEY

Cho Oyu ▲▲
Everest
[Sagarmatha]
Makalu ▲ ▲ Lhotse

Kanchenjunga ▲

INDIA

Ganges

Tibet
[CHINA]

BANGLADESH

BHUTAN

Arabian
Sea

PAKISTAN

ASIA

INDIA

NEPAL
Tibet

BHUTAN

BANGLADESH

CHINA

MYANMAR

Bay of
Bengal

INDIAN OCEAN

0 — 500 Miles
0 — 500 KM

Near the center of the Hills region lies the Kathmandu Valley. This circular valley once contained a lake. It's the largest flat area outside the Terai. The Himalayas protect the valley from icy northern winds in winter. The Mahabharat Range shields it from the heaviest rain during the summer monsoon (a strong, southerly, rain-laden wind). The valley's terrain and climate make it another important farming area. It is also home to Nepal's capital city, Kathmandu.

Nepal's Greater Himalaya region runs along its northern border. It makes up about 35 percent of Nepal's land and is sparsely populated. This very high region includes the Greater Himalayas, a range that rises from 9,843 to 29,035 feet (3,000 to 8,850 m). This region also contains Mount Everest (Sagarmartha to Nepalis), the world's highest peak. It has seven other of the world's ten highest peaks as well. These are Kanchenjunga, Lhotse, Makalu, Cho Oyu, Dhaulagiri, Manaslu, and Annapurna.

THE HIMALAYAS

The Himalayas stretch across Afghanistan, Pakistan, India, Nepal, China, and Bhutan. Their arc is about 1,500 miles (2,400 km) long and up to 250 miles (400 km) wide.

The Himalayas emerged about sixty million years ago, when the shifting Indian subcontinent crashed into the fixed Asian continent. These two landmasses are still moving toward each other. Earthquakes occur often in the region, and the mountains keep rising as India plows under Tibet.

Scientists predict that in ten million years, India will plow under Tibet an additional 112 miles (180 km). Nepal's northern and southern borders will meet, and Nepal will technically disappear.

Rivers

A complex network of streams and rivers crisscrosses Nepal. The waterways drain melting snow and ice from the Himalayas and monsoon rain from the Hills and Terai. Eventually, they all empty into the Ganges River in India.

Nepal's rivers form three main systems: the Karnali, the Narayani, and the Kosi. All begin on the Tibetan Plateau. This plateau is a vast, flat highland area north of the Himalayas.

The Karnali River in western Nepal is the nation's longest river. It is famous for its deep gorges (valleys) and swift current. It draws white-water rafters from around the world. However, it has a different effect on local residents. Along much of it, the canyons are too wide for suspension bridges, and the current is too fast for ordinary boating. As a result, the Karnali and its tributaries (feeder streams) tend to isolate the settlements along their banks.

The Narayani River cuts through central Nepal. Its mountain tributaries carve some of the world's deepest gorges. Its shallow basins connected by waterfalls are ideal for generating hydroelectricity (water-powered energy). Small steamships and timber barges navigate the lower Narayani when it's not flooded.

The Kosi River drains eastern Nepal. It has seven major tributaries. During the rainy season, the Kosi overflows its banks as it crosses the Terai in Nepal and India, dumping tons of silt there. Because this river so often floods and changes course, it has caused a lot of human suffering through the centuries. As a result, it figures prominently in both Hindu literature and regional folklore.

Climate

Nepal's climate is remarkably varied for such a small country. Two main factors influence Nepal's weather. The first is the country's terrain. The second is its monsoon (seasonal wind reversal).

Nepal's terrain is a key factor because temperature drops as altitude rises. Hills and mountains also affect the land's exposure to sunlight and wind. One side of a mountain is sunny while the other side is shady. One side is windy while the other is still.

Nepal's monsoon is another key factor because it brings air and moisture from neighboring areas. From June to September, strong winds blow northwest off the Indian Ocean's Bay of Bengal. These winds carry warm, wet air toward Nepal. As the air travels over higher and higher land, it cools. Its moisture condenses (turns from gas to liquid) and falls as rain. From December to March, strong winds blow southwest off China. These winds bring snow to the Himalayas and short rainfalls to the Hills and Terai.

Young women on the Terai use huge leaves to keep off the monsoon rains.
They carry baskets with head straps as they harvest rain-soaked fields.

The winds drop much of their moisture before they reach high elevations. As a result, Nepal is generally wetter in the lowlands and the east. It is generally drier in the highlands and the west.

The Terai has hot, humid weather during the summer monsoon. This region gets 80 percent of its rain from June to September. Summer temperatures in the Terai average 80°F (27°C) in the east and 90°F (32°C) in the drier west. Winter temperatures average around 75°F (24°C) with scattered showers. The Terai's driest season is from March to June.

In the Hills, summers are warm and rainy, and winters are chilly and dry. The Kathmandu Valley has a rainy season from June to September, a cold season from October to April, and a hot season in May and June. In January, the coldest month, temperatures range between 36° and 64°F (2° and 18°C). They sometimes reach a high of 90°F (32°C) in May and June. Higher in the Hills, summer temperatures average 54° to 61°F (12° to 16°C).

The Himalayas endure long, severe winters. In some areas, the frost never thaws. Summers are short and cool, with an average temperature of 45°F (7°C). The snow line (above which snow covers the ground year-round) begins between 12,000 and 16,000 feet (3,658 and 4,877 m). The snow line's altitude depends on how much moisture an area receives.

Flora and Fauna

Because Nepal's climate varies from tropical to arctic, the nation is home to a stunning array of plants and animals. About 7,000 different plant species live in Nepal. The country also supports a high number of animal species for its size. For example, about 180 kinds of mammals, 270 breeding bird species, 120 kinds of reptiles, and 50 amphibian species live there. The flora and fauna in any region of Nepal reflects its altitude and precipitation (rain or snow).

People have cleared much of the Terai for farming. But stands of hardwood, bamboo, and palm thrive in protected areas and on timber plantations (large farms). Sal trees are very common in this region. Their wood resembles teak, a valuable hardwood.

Elephants, rhinoceroses, leopards, tigers, deer, and crocodiles live in the forests and swamps of the Terai. This area also has a wide variety of snakes, from the small and harmless garter snake to the king cobra, the world's largest poisonous snake.

The cooler, drier climate and higher altitude of the Hills region suits a different variety of plants and animals. Pine and oak trees prevail here. Alders, laurels, walnuts, chestnuts, maples, wild cherries, firs, birches, rhododendrons, and larches are also common. In these forests live black bears, wild boars, wildcats, foxes, and a wide variety of birds.

At lower altitudes in the mountains, pine trees, firs, and birches

An **Indian rhinoceros grazes in Chitwan National Park.** This species is endangered, due largely to poachers who kill rhinos and sell their horns for use in traditional Chinese medicine.

grow. At about 13,000 feet (4,000 m), the trees give way to shrubs such as junipers and rhododendrons. Grasses, mosses, lichens, and tiny flowers also grow in the alpine tundra (treeless high-altitude zone). Snow covers the ground year-round above 16,000 feet (4,877 m). A few hardy plants, such as mosses and alpine flowers, can survive up to 20,000 feet (6,100 m). Above that no plant life exists.

Animals are plentiful in the lower mountains. This region is home to foxes, various wild goats and sheep, snow leopards, musk deer, and yaks. Bird species include snow partridges and snow cocks. Above the tree line, the most important animal is the yak, a relative of cattle and buffalo. Yaks measure about 6 feet (1.8 m) tall at the shoulder and weigh about 1,000 pounds (454 kilograms). They have short legs, long shaggy hair, and curved horns. Nepal's Himalayan region has a small population of wild yaks and a large population of tame ones (often crossbred with cattle).

Yaks are very useful to Nepal's highlanders. Yaks carry goods over mountain passes. They provide rich milk, cheese, and butter—and sometimes meat. Their hair makes a soft yarn that Nepalis knit into warm fabric. Yak droppings make good fuel too.

◉ Natural Resources

Throughout the centuries, Nepal's key natural resources have been its land, plants, and animals. Nepal has always had a mostly rural society. Its people rely heavily on the earth and its fruits for their survival. In modern times, the nation's amazing terrain and biodiversity (variety of living things) draw visitors from every corner of the world. These tourists contribute a great deal to Nepal's economy.

Nepal's energy resources are limited. It has small fossil fuel (coal, oil, and natural gas) deposits, and it does not extract these fuels. Wood and animal dung provide 87 percent of the energy Nepalis use. Imported fossil fuels and domestic hydropower provide the rest. Scientists estimate that Nepal uses less than 1 percent of its feasible hydropower. They say that if Nepal were to harness its full water-power potential, it could meet all its energy needs. It could also sell electricity to neighboring countries.

Nepal has a variety of mineral resources, but they are mostly undeveloped. The country's rugged terrain makes mining and transport very difficult. Also, most Nepalis are poor and undereducated. The population has a shortage of expertise and money needed to extract minerals. Nonetheless, mining for nonmetal minerals—especially those useful in construction—is active. Scientists believe that Nepal may have a lot of undiscovered gold, lead, and zinc. Its future metal mining is likely to focus on these three resources.

Environmental Issues

Nepal faces several serious environmental challenges. These problems are largely a result of widespread poverty and high population growth.

An ever-growing number of poor Nepalis require food, shelter, and other means of survival. To supply their needs, people cut down trees. This not only opens up farmland and pasture but also provides fuel and building material. Nepal was once rich in timber, but only 29 percent of its land remains forested. Deforestation (clearing trees) continues at a rate of 2.3 percent per year in the Hills and 1.3 percent per year in the Terai.

Deforestation has, in turn, led to other environmental problems in Nepal. Wood burning contributes to air pollution. Heavy farming depletes the soil's nutrients, leading to more clearing as people search for fertile land. Topsoil erodes (washes away) by the ton, choking rivers and lakes. Overgrazing by animals makes the erosion worse. Water quality and availability suffer. Landslides and floods increase. And as suitable habitat dwindles, so does wildlife.

Most of the trees on this hill were cut down to build and heat homes. When trees disappear so quickly, the soil quality declines and other trees die.

Poor residents of Kathmandu search **piles of trash along the Bagmati River** for usable items. Uncontrolled sewage and garbage dumping along the Bagmati have severely polluted its waters.

As Nepal's natural resources wane, Nepalis find it harder to survive in rural areas. Since the 1950s, the nation's population has steadily shifted into the cities. At the same time, Nepal has been developing its tourism industry aggressively. As more and more people move to the cities, cities struggle to manage all their garbage and sewage. And as more and more foreigners visit Nepal, they tread heavily on this beautiful—but fragile—country.

Both Nepalis and concerned outsiders are aware of these problems and are trying to solve them. For example, the government is developing laws to protect its environment. Public and private organizations are establishing programs that address both deforestation and rural poverty. And there is growing support for ecotourism, which helps Nepal earn income without destroying its natural resources.

◉ Cities

Although the population of Nepal is steadily shifting to its cities, about 86 percent of Nepalis still live in rural communities. The Kathmandu Valley, in Nepal's Hills region, is home to a large percentage of Nepal's urban population. The cities of Kathmandu and Lalitpur are the valley's major communities.

KATHMANDU (population 671,846) Legend says that King Gunakamadeva founded Kathmandu in the late A.D. 900s. The city's original name was Kantipur (city of glory). Its residents built a temple called Kasthamandap (house of wood) in the heart of town. The city's current name comes from this temple's name.

Modern Kathmandu is Nepal's capital and largest city. It is the center of the nation's administrative, cultural, and business activities. Kathmandu houses not only most of Nepal's government offices but also the palace of Nepal's royal family. It is a hub for the valley's many industries, such as carpet weaving, brick making, cement manufacturing, and food processing. It is also the center of Nepal's transportation system. Tribhuvan International Airport is located here. Kathmandu is the gateway to Nepal for tourists. Adventure seekers begin their journeys in this city. Its rich cultural heritage makes it a primary destination for most other visitors.

Kathmandu has many modern buildings, but the old section of the city still flourishes. Its narrow streets are crowded with shops and vendors. Durbar Square, Kathmandu's ancient center, remains the city's cultural focal point. Scattered around this square are some of the capital's finest temples, palaces, and other historic buildings. Within Kathmandu, on the sacred Bagmati River, lies Pashupatinath, the holiest temple for Nepali Hindus. Pilgrims (religious travelers) from all over the country come here to worship, bathe, and spend their last days.

Worshippers crowd around the Hindu temple Pashupatinath in Kathmandu.

The **Hiranya Varna Mahavihar,** also called the Golden Temple, was founded in Lalitpur in the twelfth century.

BIRATNAGAR (population 166,674) The biggest city outside the Kathmandu Valley is Biratnagar, an industrial and commercial center in the eastern Terai. Biratnagar is Nepal's second-largest city.

LALITPUR (population 162,991), founded in the A.D. 600s, is 3 miles (5 km) south of Kathmandu. It is Nepal's third-largest city. As the home of Nepal's renowned Newar craftspeople, Lalitpur is a major artistic center. It is also a mostly Buddhist city. Ornate temples, shrines, and decorative wood carvings line its narrow, winding streets. Historically, Lalitpur's economy has relied on both art and agriculture. Art is still important in modern Lalitpur, but service businesses—especially tourism—are replacing agriculture.

POKHARA (population 156,312) is Nepal's fourth-largest city. Lying 123 miles (198 km) west of Kathmandu at the foot of the Annapurna Range, Pokhara is a magnet for hikers and a regional center for handicrafts and commerce.

Visit www.vgsbooks.com for links to websites with additional information about visiting Nepal. Find out what you need to plan a mountain trek and get a glimpse of Nepal's biggest attractions.

HISTORY AND GOVERNMENT

Archaeologists have found neolithic tools (ancient tools made of polished stone) in the Kathmandu Valley. These tools show that people were living in Nepal during the last part of the Stone Age (9000 to 3500 B.C.).

The Kirata Era

The Gopalas were the first known tribe to settle in the Kathmandu Valley. The kings of this nomadic (moving with the seasons) cow-herding people were Nepal's first dynasty (family of rulers). They reigned from the 1600s to the 1400s B.C.

The Abhiras, a nomadic herding people from the Terai, eventually conquered the Gopalas. The Abhiras ruled from the 1400s to the 1300s B.C. Under this dynasty, Nepali territory expanded in all directions.

In the 1300s B.C., the Kiratas from the east conquered the Abhiras. The Kiratas ruled the Kathmandu Valley for more than one thousand years. Their civilization formed the basis for the social, religious, economic, and political development of ancient Nepal.

The Kiratas cleared land for farming by cutting and burning vegetation. They moved on every few years to open up new areas. But in the most fertile valleys, people settled permanently. In these places, a more complex civilization evolved. The most important of these sites was the Kathmandu Valley. There a trade center developed. From here the Kiratas exported woolen blankets and carpets as well as treated animal skins.

While the Kiratas ruled central Nepal, two other notable kingdoms arose nearby. One was the Videha kingdom. The other was the Sakya kingdom.

The Videha kingdom lay in the eastern Terai. Its rulers were called Janaks, and its capital was the city of Janakpur. Videha civilization was famous for its wisdom, literature, religion, and tolerance. Education of women was common there, unlike elsewhere.

The Sakya kingdom lay in the western Terai. Its capital was the city of Kapilvastu. This kingdom is famous for producing a

NEPAL'S WRITTEN HISTORY

Modern knowledge about ancient Nepal is incomplete because its people didn't keep many written records. Most of the available evidence describes events that happened in the Kathmandu Valley. Written references to this region first appeared after 1000 B.C., when the people of northern India became aware of political and social groupings in Nepal.

Some ancient Nepali works of art and architecture carry epigraphs (engraved inscriptions). The oldest known epigraph—a brief one—dates from about A.D. 100. The next-oldest one dates from the 400s. More written historical evidence, such as epigraphs and coins, survive from the fifth century onward. Oral legends and folktales also capture the flavor of life in ancient Nepal. But historians can't prove that these accounts reflect actual events.

In the 1300s, Nepalis began collecting these stories, as well as their other historical knowledge, into *vamsavalis* (written chronicles). Nepal's vamsavalis make up the most complete available account of its history. Historical records from India and China confirm many of the events described in these chronicles.

prince named Siddhartha Gautama. Guatama was born in about 563 B.C. at Lumbini, a town near Kapilvastu. As an adult, he became known as Buddha (enlightened one) and founded a religion called Buddhism. He visited the Kathmandu Valley, where he toured Hindu shrines and preached his beliefs. He converted some Kiratas from Hinduism—the area's main religion—to Buddhism.

Two centuries later, India's emperor, Asoka, became a Buddhist. As Asoka expanded his empire, he traveled widely and encouraged the spread of Buddhism. At Lumbini, Asoka erected a pillar to commemorate Buddha's birth. Asoka may also have visited the Kathmandu Valley and built four stupas (shrines) in Lalitpur.

Asoka's daughter Charumati married a Nepali prince named Devapala. Together they founded the towns of Chabahil and Deopatan. Although Asoka extended Buddhism throughout the Kathmandu Valley, he never gained power over the region. Kirata rule continued until at least the first century A.D. After that the Lichhavis took control.

The Lichhavis

The Lichhavis came to the Kathmandu Valley from India. Though historians don't know exactly how or when this family rose to power, written records show that the dynasty was firmly established by the 400s.

Under the Lichhavis, Nepal entered a golden age of arts. Indian influence was strong during this period. The Lichhavis developed a well-organized government and increased trade with both India and Tibet. They also divided Nepali society into Hindu castes (hereditary social classes). Hinduism spread alongside Buddhism, leading to the fusion of these religions in Nepal.

Manadeva I, the best-known Lichhavi king, ruled from 464 to 505. When Manadeva ascended the throne as a boy, the Thakuris—a people living in the eastern part of the realm—tried to take advantage of his inexperience. They rebelled in an attempt to gain independence. But Manadeva had superior military skills, and he suppressed the rebels. Encouraged by his success, Manadeva then marched westward with his army. He crossed the Kali Gandaki River and defeated the people of Mallapuri.

The Thakuris

In 602 Amsuvarma began the Thakuri dynasty. He inherited the throne from his father-in-law, the Lichhavi king Shivadeva I. Amsuvarma was a devoted Hindu, but he also promoted Buddhist teachings.

During this period, Tibet grew very powerful. Under King Srong-brtsan-sgam-po, Tibet conquered a large portion of central Asia, including parts of China and the Himalayas.

Likely recognizing Tibet's power over Nepal, Amsuvarma arranged for his daughter Bhrikuti to marry the Tibetan king. Bhrikuti brought Buddhist artifacts with her to Tibet. Along with the king's second wife (a Chinese princess who also was Buddhist), Bhrikuti converted Srong-brtsan-sgam-po and much of his realm to Buddhism.

This change in spirituality was just one lasting effect of Tibet's new relationship with Nepal. Nepal changed Tibetan culture in other ways too. For example, Indian

This statue of Tibetan king **Srong-brtsan-sgam-po** celebrates his conversion to Buddhism. The statue was made in Tibet around the time of his death in 649 or 650.

THE RISE OF TANTRISM

The religious tolerance of Lichhavi and Thakuri kings led to the development of a new spiritual practice called Tantrism. A blend of Buddhism, Hinduism, and folk beliefs, Tantrism may have arisen in Nepal as early as the 600s. The new religion expanded Hindu beliefs and practices and inspired a Buddhist trend called Vajrayana.

Tantrists opposed the life of self-examination encouraged by Buddhists. They believed concrete action and direct experience were the best means to achieve divine bliss (ultimate happiness). The movement greatly influenced both the people of Nepal and their art, which often depicted physical pleasures.

forms of writing and literature entered Tibet from Nepal. So did Nepali art and architecture.

Nepal also increased its contact with China during the 600s and 700s. In 646 the Chinese established their first embassy in the Kathmandu Valley. Nepali architecture spread to China at this time. Nepal's most important architectural export was the pagoda, a multistoried tower with upward-curving roofs between levels.

Chinese travelers to Nepal marveled at the legacy of Amsuvarma. Xuanzang, a Buddhist monk who made a famous pilgrimage from China to India, admired Amsuvarma's palace. He wrote that it stood seven stories tall and was covered with gems and pearls. Golden dragon fountains surrounded the palace, and the king sat on a lion-shaped throne.

Good relations between China and Nepal improved Nepal's standing in India. Nepal was a vital trade link between India and China. Indians acknowledged Amsuvarma as a Kshatriya, a member of the Hindu warrior caste. (At that time, Kshatriya was India's second highest of four castes.) Nepal strengthened its political connections with India through marriage, just as it had done with Tibet.

Few historical records remain from the 800s through the 1100s, Nepal's dark age. The surviving sources show that during this period, internal conflict and foreign invasions constantly disrupted Nepali society. The vamsavalis also describe a string of natural disasters, such as earthquakes and epidemics. Despite the turmoil of these centuries, trade flourished and settlements grew along the trade routes.

A ruler named Gunakamadeva founded the city of Kantipur (modern Kathmandu) in the late 900s, at a site where a small community already existed. He also introduced three major Hindu festivals and built the Kasthamandap temple, from which Kathmandu would later take its name.

After Gunakamadeva's reign, the people of the Kathmandu Valley reorganized into the separate kingdoms of Kantipur, Lalitpur, and Bhaktapur. Joint rule by two or more kings became a common practice among Thakuri leaders.

○▷ The Mallas

According to the vamsavalis, in about 1200, a Thakuri king named Arideva was wrestling when he heard news of his son's birth. He bestowed the title *malla* (wrestler) on the infant, thus beginning the Malla dynasty. Although the name Malla suggests conflict, the Malla era proved to be mostly peaceful.

The Malla kings claimed to be incarnations (physical embodiments) of Vishnu, the Hindu god of preservation. They strictly followed Hindu religious practices. They also tolerated Buddhism, which was widespread among the general population.

The Malla era peaked under King Jayasthiti Malla, in the late 1300s. He unified the Kathmandu Valley, which had been in a state of civil war. He also introduced legal codes and expanded the Hindu caste system to include the whole population. Occupation, family status, and other social criteria determined an individual's assignment to one of dozens of castes.

Residents of the Kathmandu Valley became known as the Newar during this period. Newar society was an ethnic mixture of the valley's original inhabitants, Himalayan peoples from the north and east, and Indians from the south and west. Its culture combined elements of all these traditions.

Newar culture flourished during the Malla era. Skilled Newar artists and craftspeople developed a distinctive style that survives in the architecture, wood carving, and sculpture of modern Nepal. Newari became the language of the king's court.

After Jayasthiti Malla's death in 1395, his sons divided the kingdom and ruled cooperatively. The Malla kingdom began to decline during this

A thirteenth-century Newar artist from Lalitpur carved this **statue of a *garuda*,** a creature that appears in both Hindu and Buddhist mythology. The garuda has a man's body with an eagle's beak, wings, and talons.

period. Fragmented authority created administrative chaos. It also reduced accountability and encouraged scheming among government officials. Eventually the last surviving son, Jyotir Malla, ruled on his own from 1408 to 1428.

After Jyotir Malla's death in 1428, his son Yaksya Malla reigned until 1482. Prosperity and stability returned to the region as Yaksya Malla improved the lives of his people. Art and literature thrived. The king ordered the construction of many temples and shrines—both Hindu and Buddhist—as well as public works such as canals. He expanded the kingdom in all directions.

Yaksya Malla arranged for his sons to divide the kingdom and rule cooperatively after his death. This act broke the unity he had established. Eventually the realm separated into three smaller kingdoms. The Kathmandu Valley continued to flourish economically and artistically. The Malla dynasty, however, slowly crumbled under political rivalries over the next three centuries.

During the 1400s and 1500s, events outside the Kathmandu Valley grew more important to Nepal's development as a nation. Muslim armies invaded India from southwestern Asia and began converting Hindus to Islam. (Islam is a religion founded by the Arab prophet Muhammad in the 600s.) As this new dynasty, the Mughals, conquered more and more of India, India's Hindu princes fled to western Nepal. The Mughals also raided the Kathmandu Valley, but they didn't remain there.

The exiled princes established more than forty small domains in central and western Nepal. Each of these kingdoms operated independently. They continually fought with one another. Eventually the Gurkha kingdom in central Nepal grew very powerful under the Shah dynasty.

The Shahs of Gurkha

The Shah dynasty began with Dravya Shah. He ruled Gurkha from 1559 to 1570. Over the next two centuries, this dynasty gradually expanded Gurkha territory.

In the mid-1700s, Prithvi Narayan Shah began a major conquest of the Himalayan region. A fierce and resourceful warrior-king, he overpowered Gurkha's neighbors, including the three powerful Kathmandu Valley kingdoms. Thanks to political instability among the Malla rulers, Prithvi Narayan Shah controlled the entire valley by 1769.

Prithvi Narayan Shah moved his capital from Gurkha to Kathmandu. He called his new realm the Kingdom of Nepal. Composed of peoples from the Terai, the Hills, and the Himalayas, this kingdom laid the social and geographical foundation for modern Nepal.

Meanwhile, throughout the 1700s, the British had spread their colonial empire into India. Prithvi Narayan Shah restricted trade with the British in India to prevent British colonial interest in Nepal. He also banished many people he considered threatening to national unity. These included foreign traders, missionaries (religious teachers), and musicians and artists influenced by northern India.

Prithvi Narayan Shah's descendants continued Gurkha expansion. By the end of the 1700s, Nepal's territory extended along the Himalayas from southern Kashmir in northwestern India to Sikkim in northeastern India—roughly twice the size of modern Nepal.

● Foreign Conflicts

In the late 1770s, Nepal became embroiled in a conflict with Tibet. At issue were currency exchange rates, control of mountain passes, and taxation of goods traveling between Tibet and India.

Nepali troops invaded Tibet in 1788 and 1791. China—whose powerful Qing dynasty formally controlled Tibet—ordered Nepali troops to leave. When they refused, China sent about seventy thousand soldiers to Tibet. The Chinese army soon conquered the Nepali forces and entered Nepal. Nepal agreed to return Tibetan territory; give up its trading privileges in Tibet; and make a payment to Beijing, China's capital, every five years.

As Tibet blocked Nepal on one side, Nepal's western neighbors stood strong on another. Nepal turned its attention southward. At the same time, the British were moving northward in India. When the British East India Company (the United Kingdom's colonial agency in Asia) extended India's territory to Nepal's border, Nepal angered the British by raiding India. Nepal also refused to establish trade contracts and diplomatic relations with the British.

This painting shows a **captain of the British East India Company** as an enlightened person in company with the Buddha. A Lalitpur artist made it in 1803 to decorate a box containing a Buddhist manuscript.

These **Gurkha soldiers** fought for the British Army when Indian rebels mutinied against British rule in 1857.

BRITISH GURKHAS

Although Nepal lost the Anglo-Nepali War, its troops had greatly impressed the British. The British recruited Gurkha soldiers into the British Army. In return for this contribution, in the late 1800s, the British restored much of Nepal's territory. As a result, Nepal assumed its modern shape and size. And the British military has included Gurkha soldiers ever since.

The British wanted to meet to discuss dividing the territories along the India-Nepal border. Nepal refused to participate. So in 1814, Great Britain declared war and sent troops to occupy the territories. Nepal resisted for two years. But by early 1816, Nepal's army was outnumbered, outgunned, and outmaneuvered. To make matters worse, Sikkim was pushing Nepal from the east too. In March 1816, Nepal and Great Britain signed the Treaty of Segauli, ending the Anglo-Nepali War. This treaty shrank Nepal's holdings in the west, south, and east. It also established diplomatic relations between Great Britain and Nepal.

The Ranas

During the early 1800s, a series of weak Shah kings made the post of prime minister an increasingly powerful position. By the late 1830s, competition for the position had become bloody. Assassins often murdered rivals.

In 1846 an army commander named Jung Bahadur became prime minister by killing many of his opponents and driving several thousand Nepalis into exile. He filled the government with relatives and made the position of prime minister hereditary. He and other family members added Rana (a title denoting royalty and military glory) to their names and stripped the king of his power.

In 1850 Jung Bahadur embarked on a ten-month trip to Europe. He visited Great Britain and France, both to broaden his horizons and to strengthen his contacts there. Back at home, he began a strict policy of isolation for all other Nepalis. Foreigners rarely gained admission into the country. Those who did visit had very little contact with Nepalis. This arrangement prevented locals from learning about conditions and developments in the rest of the world.

The Ranas held complete control in Nepal for more than a century. Their rule brought a few benefits, such as excellent relations with Great Britain, better relations with China, and sweeping legal reforms. Most importantly, the Ranas preserved Nepal's independence while nearly all its neighbors became European colonies. But the Ranas did very little for Nepal's overall development. They constantly fought each other for power and stored up personal wealth. Meanwhile, their lavish lifestyle contrasted sharply with the poverty of most Nepalis.

Anti-Rana Revolution

During the 1930s and 1940s, opposition to Rana rule grew. In the late 1940s, two anti-Rana political parties formed. They joined forces to form the Nepali Congress Party. King Tribhuvan, the powerless Shah monarch, secretly supported this movement to overthrow the Ranas.

Meanwhile, India had struggled to gain independence from Great Britain. It won independence in 1947 shortly after World War II (1939–1945). India's newly won independence aided Nepalis' struggle for a more open society. The Ranas had enjoyed friendly relations with British India. But when the British turned India's government over to the Indians, it changed dramatically. The Ranas suddenly faced a powerful neighbor that pressured Nepal to make democratic reforms—as India itself was doing.

In February 1950, during talks with Indian prime minister Jawaharlal Nehru, the Ranas agreed to establish a two-house legislature (lawmaking body). But they delayed other political reforms, and public uprisings broke out in the fall of 1950.

By December 1950, Nepal's government troops had joined the rebellion. Many members of the Rana family encouraged the prime minister to negotiate with the Indian government, which supported Nepal's political revolution. In January 1951, the Rana prime minister agreed to introduce several democratic reforms, pardon all political

King Mahendra and his wife, Queen Indra, share the throne of Nepal during his coronation ceremony in 1956.

prisoners, and restore King Tribhuvan to the throne. The king's return signaled the end of the Rana dynasty.

Return of the King

The early years of post-Rana rule were unstable. For eight years, the government alternated between administrations appointed by the king and direct rule by the king himself. Infighting weakened Nepal's political parties.

After King Tribhuvan died in 1955, his son Mahendra succeeded him. In 1959 King Mahendra enacted Nepal's first constitution. The document preserved the king's ultimate power, but it also created a bicameral (two-house) legislature with a publicly elected lower house. The Nepali Congress Party (NCP) won two-thirds of the lower house seats. Its leader, Bishweshwar Prasad (B. P.) Koirala, became Nepal's first elected prime minister.

Never a true supporter of democracy, King Mahendra was quick to criticize Koirala's government. The king denounced the rivalries among the political parties. He decried Nepal's ongoing unrest and violence. He accused the NCP leaders of corruption and failure to provide national leadership or maintain law and order. In 1960 he dissolved the elected government and jailed its leaders.

King Mahendra claimed that Nepal needed a political system closer to Nepali traditions. In 1962 he enacted a new constitution that established a partyless *panchayat* (village council) system. The panchayat system let Nepali voters elect village councils. These councils then elected members of regional panchayats, which in turn elected representatives to the National Panchayat.

At the national level, this system gave the king a great deal of power. The National Panchayat could not criticize the king or the panchayat system, introduce budget bills without royal approval, or enact laws without the king's blessing. The king was military commander in chief. He appointed and dismissed supreme court judges, and he could change any judicial decision. He could amend the constitution anytime.

Though King Mahendra did not tolerate political opposition, his government gave Nepal a much-needed economic boost. He encouraged tourism and built roads and hydroelectric power stations. He also initiated land and legal reforms. Public health programs wiped out malaria (a deadly disease spread by mosquitoes) in the Terai, making this region more suitable for settlement and farming. Thanks to many of these changes, Nepal's agricultural output increased.

When King Mahendra died in 1972, his son Birendra took the throne. King Birendra continued the programs his father had established.

Struggle for Democracy

Despite the Shahs' efforts to improve economic and social conditions in Nepal, life was still very hard for most Nepalis. As they learned more about the outside world and compared Nepal to other countries, discontent grew.

Throughout the 1970s, opposition groups organized around the nation. They encouraged people to express their displeasure with the panchayat system. This decade saw many student demonstrations against the system and for human rights.

In 1979 King Birendra called for a national referendum (vote). He invited Nepalis to either support the panchayat system with democratic reforms or reject it in favor of a multiparty system. In May 1980, two-thirds of Nepalis turned out to vote. The panchayat system won by a very slim margin. The king carried out the promised reforms by amending the constitution.

Most members of Nepal's various political parties rejected the amended constitution. They also boycotted (refused to participate in) elections throughout the 1980s. Both the panchayat system and opposition politics began to disintegrate due to infighting.

In 1990 the political parties pressed King Birendra for change. Nepal's various Communist parties joined to form the United Left Front. (Communism is a political theory supporting community ownership of all property.) The United Left Front then allied with the NCP. Together, these groups launched Jana Andolan (the People's Movement). Thousands of Nepalis marched in pro-democracy rallies in Kathmandu and other towns. Police tried to break up the demonstrations, arresting protesters and firing on crowds of people. Street fighting between the police and demonstrators claimed many lives.

King Birendra responded by lifting the ban on political parties and by agreeing to talks with the Nepali Congress Party and the United Left Front. The opposition's demands included scrapping the panchayat system, dramatically revising the constitution, releasing political prisoners, and forming an interim government to rule until a new round of elections.

In April 1990, an interim (temporary) government made up of NCP members, Communist representatives, royal appointees, and independents took charge of Nepal. This government enacted a new constitution in November 1990. It guaranteed basic human rights and established Nepal as a parliamentary democracy under a constitutional monarch. Nepal's king had previously had ultimate control of the nation. When Nepal became a parliamentary monarchy, its king remained head of state (chief public representative), but a prime minister became head of government (chief decision-making authority).

International observers judged the elections that followed, in May 1991, as free and fair. The NCP won a majority of seats, thereby earning the right to form Nepal's government. This event seemed to mark a new beginning for democracy in Nepal.

Maoist Insurgency

In mid-1994, Nepal's parliament (legislature) dissolved amid Nepali Congress Party quarreling. Later that year, a general election gave no party a majority. The Communist Party of Nepal (Unified Marxist-Leninist), also called CPN-UML, won the most votes. This made Nepal the world's first Communist monarchy. For the next five years, Nepal had a series of unstable coalition (cooperative) governments. This period also spawned an insurgency (revolt) by Nepali Maoists. (Maoists are people who follow the Communist ideas of China's Mao Zedong, which focus on the importance of rural peasants.)

In February 1996, the Communist Party of Nepal (Maoist), also known as CPNM, launched a campaign of violence called the People's War. Though CPNM doesn't represent all Nepal's Communists, it became the nation's most powerful Communist group. CPNM killed, tortured, bombed, kidnapped, and bullied civilians, police, and public officials in more than two-thirds of the nation's districts. The conflict, also known as the Nepali Civil War, dragged on year after year.

A **Maoist woman speaks to thousands of Nepalis** in a remote village in 2001. Maoists demanded that the king distribute Nepal's wealth equally.

In the 1999 general elections, the Nepali Congress Party regained a majority of parliament seats. An NCP prime minister once again headed a government made up of more allies than foes. But Nepal's pattern of short-lived administrations persisted. The years 1999, 2000, and 2001 each brought a new prime minister.

The monarchy had troubles of its own during this time. Disagreement within the royal family over the crown prince's choice of bride turned deadly. (The crown prince is the heir expected to be the next king.) On June 1, 2001, King Birendra's son Dipendra shot and killed his father, his mother, his brother, his sister, and five other relatives before turning his gun on himself. Dipendra lingered in a coma for a few days, during which he was technically Nepal's king. After his death on June 4, Birendra's brother Gyanendra became king.

Nepal's political chaos continued. The government and the Maoists held a series of peace talks in late 2001. But these talks failed, and the Maoists resumed their violent insurgency. King Gyanendra then declared—and the parliament approved—a state of emergency. In 2002 the king dissolved the parliament, removed the prime minister, and called off the November parliamentary elections. For the next few years, the king ruled Nepal via a puppet (false) democracy. These years saw ongoing violence and growing opposition to Nepal's ineffective, undemocratic government.

The Struggle Continues

By February 2005, King Gyanendra had seized full control of the nation. In response, Nepal's political parties and Maoists began working together to reduce the king's power. Nepalis turned out by the thousands to demonstrate for democracy.

Faced by this united front, the king reluctantly reinstated the parliament in early 2006. A seven-party coalition took over the government and stripped most of the king's powers. Soon the new government and the Maoists independently declared cease-fires (an end to fighting). Negotiations led to a full peace agreement in November 2006. The 2006 agreement created an interim constitution that promotes democratic principles. It also set up an interim parliament with guaranteed Maoist participation. The agreement scheduled elections for a new Constituent Assembly (constitution-writing body) to occur in mid-2007.

The Nepali Civil War raged for ten years (1996–2006). It eventually killed more than fourteen thousand people and drove about six hundred thousand people from their homes, forcing them to seek shelter elsewhere in Nepal. More than two million additional people fled to India.

These elections didn't happen. Instead, in mid-2007, the Maoists withdrew from the interim government, demanding that the monarchy be abolished before the elections. In December 2007, all parties agreed to abolish the monarchy after the elections. The Maoists rejoined the interim government, which went on to reschedule the delayed elections for April 2008.

On April 10, 2008, Nepal held its long-awaited elections. Though a few disturbances marred the occasion, international observers judged the elections free and fair. In May, results indicated victory for Nepal's Maoists. They won more seats than any other party, but not an overall majority (more than half the seats).

Government

Nepal's government has changed dramatically since the 1950s. Before 1990 it was an absolute monarchy. Nepal's king served as both head of state and head of government. He had ultimate control of the nation. In 1990 Nepal became a parliamentary monarchy. Its king remained head of state, but a prime minister became head of the government, which included a two-chamber parliament. During the Nepali Civil War, the balance of power shifted toward parliament as Nepalis grew disillusioned with the monarchy. In 2006 all members of the parlia-

Maoist leader **Pushpa Kamal Dahal** accepts garlands of flowers during a victory rally after his party won the most votes in the 2008 elections.

ment voted to strip most of the king's powers. Shortly thereafter it enacted an interim constitution, which outlined a plan and principles for forming a new democratic government.

In the early twenty-first century, Nepal's government was still transforming. In 2007 Nepal's political parties agreed to abolish the monarchy and create a republic with the prime minister as head of state. This agreement required approval by more than half of the Constituent Assembly members elected in 2008. In May this approval was expected, and Maoist leader Pushpa Kamal Dahal (better known by his war name, Prachanda) was poised to lead the new government of Nepal.

Visit www.vgsbooks.com for links to websites with additional information about the history and government of Nepal. View the results of the 2008 elections, and watch as Nepal sets aside centuries of royal rule.

THE PEOPLE

Over thousands of years, various peoples migrated to Nepal from the north, south, east, and west. This history has laid a rich human mosaic over Nepal's varied terrain. Most ethnic groups live at particular altitudes in specific geographic pockets. Deep valleys and high ridges tend to divide Nepalis into many small, relatively isolated communities. This pattern persists in the early twenty-first century despite growing urbanization, improving transportation and communication, and increasing social mobility.

◉ Ethnic Groups

Experts estimate that Nepal has a total of more than sixty ethnic groups. The groups belong to one of two larger groups: Indo-Nepalis or Tibeto-Nepalis. Indo-Nepalis' ancestors came from the south and west. Tibeto-Nepalis' ancestors came from the north and east.

INDO-NEPALIS form a majority of Nepal's population. This group

includes the Paharis, the Newars, and the Terai Indians, as well as many others. Indo-Nepalis are mainly Hindu. They organize their society according to the Hindu caste system.

Castes form a ladder of religious and social rank among Hindus. Nepal's caste system consists of four main classes. These classes, from top to bottom, are the Brahmans (priests), Kshatriyas (warriors), Vaishyas (merchants), and Sudras (laborers). Nepalis divide these classes into a total of thirty-six castes. The full system of rank, heredity, occupation, ritual, and interaction within and among castes is very complex. It also varies by region and by ethnic group.

The Pahari live in Nepal's Hills region. They have mostly Indian ancestry, but they have intermarried with some Tibeto-Nepali groups. Most Paharis belong to high castes, and this group tends to dominate Nepal's government. However, Paharis aren't necessarily wealthy. Most own small farms, where they grow grain and raise a few animals.

The Newar speak a Tibeto-Burman language and have Tibetan

Young Newar women carry traditional oil lamps during a New Year's celebration in Kathmandu. The Newar new year begins in April.

ancestors. But centuries of close contact with India have placed them in the Indo-Nepali group. The Newar have a very distinctive culture, with well-developed styles of literature, architecture, religion, and art. The Newar live primarily in the Kathmandu Valley. Although some Newars are farmers, traditionally they are traders and craftspeople. Because they're concentrated in the Kathmandu Valley, the Newar have historically played an important role in Nepali society.

Although most of the Indians living in the Terai are Nepali citizens, culturally they are more closely related to the people of India's Ganges Plain than they are to other Nepali ethnic groups. The Tharu make up the largest group of Terai Indians. They also inhabit the neighboring Indian state of Uttar Pradesh. Most Tharus live in tightly knit communities and farm rice. The Tharu have lived in Nepal longer than most other ethnic groups, but they rank very low in Nepal's caste system.

Nepal has legally outlawed the caste system. It prohibits caste discrimination and permits marriages among people of different castes. Even so, this ancient tradition is still strong in Nepal. And because a majority of Nepalis practice it, the caste system still affects both Hindus and non-Hindus.

TIBETO-NEPALIS form a minority of Nepal's population. They live mainly in the Hills and Himalaya regions. The high Himalayas isolate many Tibeto-Nepali ethnic groups.

Some Tibeto-Nepali groups—such as the Tamang, Magar, Gurung, Rai, and Limbu—have lived in Nepal for centuries. Others, such as a number of Bhotia, arrived as recently as the 1950s, when China took control of Tibet.

Each Tibeto-Nepali group mostly lives together in a particular area, but small numbers are usually scattered around other parts of Nepal too. Most Tibeto-Nepalis earn just enough to survive through farming and raising livestock. Those living in the higher mountains are seminomadic. That is, they move their herds back and forth from high pastures in the summer to lower, warmer lands in the winter. Most Tibeto-Nepalis are Buddhists, but many have also adopted Hindu practices through their contact with Indo-Nepalis.

The Tamang live in villages in eastern and central Nepal. They work mainly as tenant farmers, load carriers, and woodcutters. Villagers own some land jointly, and an official collects taxes on privately owned property. A village priest performs seasonal agricultural rites. Large Tamang towns generally have Buddhist temples.

Most Magars are farmers who live in the central and western Hills. Originally Tibetan Buddhists, many Magars have accepted some Hindu beliefs and practices. The Gurung generally live higher in the mountains than do the Magar. They are shepherds as well as farmers, often depending mostly on their herds for a living. Some are successful businesspeople around the city of Pokhara. Although many Gurung are Buddhists, those living at lower elevations in the southern portions of Gurung territory have adopted Hinduism as well.

Anthropologists believe the Rai and Limbu peoples descended from the ancient Kiratas. Both

A **Gurung man** from central Nepal holds a baby girl on his shoulders.

GENETIC ADAPTATIONS

Some Nepali ethnic groups have inherited physical traits that help them survive in harsh environments. In Nepal's lowest and highest regions, the Tharu and Sherpa peoples thrive while others struggle.

The Terai was once a risky place to live. Teeming mosquitoes there spread malaria. Tharus have lived in the Terai for thousands of years. Over time they've adapted to their environment by developing a genetic resistance to malaria. They had the Terai to themselves until pesticides made it livable for others.

The high Himalayas are hazardous for many reasons. One is the low level of oxygen in the air. The Sherpa people have lived at high altitudes for a very long time. Their bodies have adapted to breathing air with less oxygen. Their chests are large, giving them great lung capacity. And their blood contains a high concentration of red blood cells, which can carry a lot of oxygen.

Lowlanders who visit high-altitude cities, such as Kathmandu, feel short of breath. Sherpas, by contrast, live twice that high with no breathing problems. Mountain climbers often need to carry oxygen tanks. Sherpa mountaineers don't, even atop Mount Everest.

groups live in the eastern hills. Limbu villages lie close to Nepal's border with the Indian state of Sikkim. Rai villages lie west of Limbu territory. Most Rais and Limbus practice subsistence farming (growing just enough food to feed their families) and follow both Hinduism and Buddhism.

The Bhotia, or northern border peoples, usually live at elevations above 9,000 feet (2,743 m). Their culture, language, and Buddhist practices are very similar to those of Tibetans. They farm small plots of land in the high Himalayas, raise sheep and yaks, and participate in long-distance trade. Traders sell mountain herbs and spices, woolen scarves, leather goods, and jewelry. After Nepal opened to foreign tourists in the 1950s, some Bhotia groups—especially the Sherpa—gained fame as guides and porters (baggage carriers) on mountain-climbing expeditions.

Sherpa men carry heavy packs through the mountains with ease.

Population

Nepal is home to almost 28 million people. The population is growing about 1.9 percent per year. Researchers expect the population to exceed 42 million by 2050—an increase of 53 percent.

Nepal's government views its population growth rate as too high. To control this growth, the government has made family planning a key part of national health services. The family planning program's goals are to help people space and/or limit their children, prevent unwanted pregnancies, educate adolescents, empower women, and improve overall reproductive health. Nepal aims to reduce its total fertility rate from an average of 4 children per woman in 2001 to 2 children per woman in 2017.

Nepal's overall population density is 489 people per square mile (189 people per sq. km). It is in the top 25 percent of the world's most crowded nations. Compared to its south Asian neighbors, however, Nepal's population density is moderate. Nepal is more crowded than Bhutan and China but less crowded than India and Bangladesh.

Most Nepalis live in the Hills and the Terai. Mountains cover 35 percent of Nepal's total land area but contain only 7 percent of the nation's population. By contrast, the Hills cover 42 percent of the land and contain 44 percent of the population. The Terai covers 23 percent of Nepal's land and contains 49 percent of the population.

About 86 percent of the population lives in rural areas, while 14 percent of Nepalis live in cities. The most densely populated area is the Kathmandu Valley, which is home to two of Nepal's largest cities as well as several smaller ones. The southeastern Terai is almost as crowded as the Kathmandu Valley.

WATER, WATER, EVERYWHERE . . .

Nepal has dozens of rivers fed by melting Himalayan ice and snow. But only about 20 percent of Nepalis have access to safe water because public supply systems are underdeveloped. Impure water carries bacteria (germs) that cause intestinal infections. These infections in turn decrease people's ability to absorb nutrition and fight disease.

Poverty

Nepal is one of the poorest countries in the world. Despite a recent decline in Nepal's number of urban poor people, poverty is still widespread. About 40 percent of Nepalis struggle to meet their basic food, clothing, and shelter needs.

Rural poverty is a major problem in Nepal. Most people live in the countryside and depend on subsistence farming for survival. Rural poor people are generally landless or have very small properties. Many Nepalis rely on farm plots that are too small to meet their needs. Productivity is low because of limited access to modern farming methods, ongoing war, poor soil and climate in some areas, and environmental problems such as erosion and flooding. Widespread illiteracy (inability to read, write, and do simple math) and large families make it hard for many Nepalis to improve their conditions.

Life in rural Nepal is a constant struggle for survival. Poor nutrition is rampant. Most households have little or no access to health care, education, clean drinking water, or sanitation. Those who suffer the most are the lowest castes, indigenous peoples, women, and children.

Health

As a result of rural poverty, many Nepalis suffer from hunger and live in substandard housing. Malnutrition and poor sanitation lead to many diseases and to early death. The average Nepali can expect to live only 63 years. Conditions that are rare or treatable in many other nations—such as leprosy, tuberculosis, measles, asthma, pneumonia, and diarrhea—are common and deadly in Nepal.

Nepal has a limited HIV/AIDS epidemic. About sixty-two thousand Nepalis are living with the virus. But the infection rate is rising. AIDS could be Nepal's leading cause of death by 2010 if its infection rate keeps growing.

Reproduction is dangerous for women in Nepal. The nation's rates of infant mortality and maternal mortality are among the worst in southern Asia. In Nepal 48 out of every 1,000 babies die before the age of one year. For every 10,000 women in pregnancy or childbirth, 28 women die.

Nepal faces a pressing need for better public health systems. These include not only safer drinking water and better sanitation (sewage and garbage management) but also expanded medical facilities. Nepal has only 2 doctors and 50 hospital beds for every 10,000 people.

Education

Education in Nepal improved greatly during the late twentieth century. In the early 1950s, only about 5 percent of Nepalis older than six years were literate. And only a few thousand children from the richest families attended school. In 1971 the Nepali government introduced a new education plan. This ongoing plan focuses on building schools and adding teachers every year.

Children gather at an outdoor school in the valley below Mount Everest.

The additional schools and teachers in turn have lifted Nepal's literacy and enrollment rates. By 2001 the literacy rate was 54 percent. Primary school enrollment stood at 81 percent. Lower secondary enrollment was 40 percent, and secondary school enrollment was 26 percent.

Nepal's formal public education system consists of four levels. The nation's twenty-five thousand primary schools serve children in grades one through five. More than seven thousand lower secondary schools offer grades six through eight. More than four thousand secondary schools serve grades nine and ten. About one thousand higher secondary schools—a new feature of Nepali education—offer grades eleven and twelve.

Although access to university education has been expanding, Nepal's universities serve less than 1 percent of the population. Higher education is available at five institutions: Tribhuvan University, Mahendra Sanskrit University, Kathmandu University, Pokhara University, and Purvanchal University. These universities run a total of about 250 campuses around the country.

Nepal has also developed an informal education system. This system aims to increase literacy among adults and entice children into formal schooling. Since 1992 nearly one million people have gained literacy through Nepal's informal education programs.

Visit www.vgsbooks.com for links to websites with additional information about the people of Nepal. Try out some of the languages spoken in Nepal. Learn about the lives of Sherpa guides and other Nepali ethnic groups.

CULTURAL LIFE

▶ Religion

Hinduism is Nepal's official religion. Nepali law, however, prohibits religious discrimination. Nepal's history of religious tolerance goes back more than two thousand years. As a result, spiritual beliefs and practices vary widely and often mingle. Blending of Hinduism and Buddhism (Nepal's two main religions) is especially common. Many Nepalis blend one or both of these religions with traditional animist beliefs too.

About 81 percent of Nepalis call themselves Hindus. About 11 percent consider themselves Buddhists. Of the remaining 8 percent, half are Kirata (animists) and half are Muslim (followers of Islam). These statistics mask the large impact of Buddhism and animism on Nepal's culture. Nepalis revere Buddhist and Hindu temples equally, and they celebrate the festivals of both religions. Most Nepalis regard their nation as equally Hindu and Buddhist. And most Nepalis follow some animist practices too.

Hinduism is a religion based on four ancient texts called the Vedas, compiled in about 1200 B.C. Each Veda is a collection of hymns, prayers, and rituals. Unlike other major world religions, Hinduism has no single founder. In Hinduism, divine power takes the shape of three main gods: Brahma, the creator; Vishnu, the preserver; and Shiva, the destroyer. Individual Hindus choose their own forms of worship.

Though Hindu customs and beliefs vary around the world and even within Nepal, all Hindus share a few basic concepts. One of these is karma, the belief in consequences for every action. Another basic Hindu concept is reincarnation (rebirth of the soul after death, into a new body). Karma continues through many cycles of rebirths as the consequences of human actions play out. Only when a soul finally sees beyond earthly desires can it escape the cycle of rebirth and reunite with the divine.

Buddhism is a religion founded by Siddhartha Gautama in the sixth century B.C. Siddhartha Gautama, who was born a Hindu prince, began

A Nepali woman spins **prayer wheels at a Buddhist temple** in a mountain village. Buddhists chant prayers while turning these wood or metal cylinders.

teaching Buddhist principles after he had given up worldly life and had meditated for six years. This experience led him to enlightenment (the absence of desire and suffering), and he became known as Buddha (enlightened one).

Buddhism either accepts or reinterprets many basic Hindu concepts, including karma and reincarnation. It teaches that desire causes suffering and that eliminating desire can end sorrow. It offers the Eightfold Path, a practical guide to wisdom, ethical conduct, and mental development. This path leads to the end of desire—and entrance into nirvana, a state of bliss and selfless enlightenment. Any Buddhist who reaches enlightenment is called Buddha. Some Buddhist sects encourage Buddhas to postpone entering nirvana in order to help others. These holy people are called bodhisattvas.

Animism is Nepal's oldest spiritual practice. In Nepal, animism takes the form of the Kirata religion. It involves the worship of mountain gods, spirits of diseases, ancestral spirits, and local gods. Animists entrust shamans (priests) to communicate with supernatural beings. Most Nepalis—Hindus and Buddhists alike—incorporate some aspects of animism into their daily lives. Indeed, almost all of Nepal's ethnic groups have shamans.

This traveling shaman provides medical care as well as spiritual guidance to Nepalis in remote areas.

While Hinduism and Buddhism focus on philosophical issues, animism offers a way to deal with practical problems, such as misfortune and sickness. For example, many Nepalis believe that supernatural beings cause certain illnesses and that only a shaman can determine which spirit has caused a particular problem. A shaman may prescribe rituals or herbal remedies to lure a problematic spirit from someone's body.

Islam means "submission to the will of Allah" in the Arabic language. *Allah* is the word for "God." Muslims in Nepal, as elsewhere, believe that Allah gave messages to his prophet (spiritual spokesperson) Muhammad through the angel Gabriel. The holy scriptures of the Quran contain these messages. This monotheistic (one god) religion shares roots with the Jewish and Christian religions. These three major world religions arose in the same part of the world.

Muslims strive to fulfill five central duties of faith. These are known as the five pillars of Islam: declaring faith in Allah and his prophet; praying five times daily; giving charity; fasting from sunrise to sunset during the holy month of Ramadan; and making a pilgrimage to the holy city of Mecca once in a lifetime, if possible. Friday is the holy day of the week for Muslims. Men go to the mosque to hear teachings and to pray. Women pray at home or in separate parts of the mosque.

▶ Language

Nepal's official language is Nepali. Nepali is an Indo-Aryan language, along with other southern Asian languages such as Hindi and Bengali. Modern Indo-Aryan languages come from Sanskrit (an ancient Indian language), much as modern European languages come from Latin (an ancient Roman language). Written Nepali uses the

This **fragment of a Sanskrit manuscript** uses Devanagari script.

Devanagari script. The script reads from left to right, with a top line connecting letters within a word. The Nepali Devanagari alphabet has eleven vowels and thirty-three consonants. The alphabet is phonetic—each letter represents only one sound.

Nepali is the first language (mother tongue) for 49 percent of Nepal's people. It is the second language of many more. The population has a total of ninety-two different mother tongues. Most are local languages, not foreign ones such as Chinese or English. Besides Nepali, eleven other local languages are spoken by more than 1 percent of the population.

Literature

Until the late 1900s, few Nepalis could read. As a result, Nepal has a long, rich tradition of oral literature. For many centuries, villagers have listened to storytellers, who keep alive legends far older than the written word in Nepal.

Throughout most of Nepal's history, its written literature has targeted a very small elite class. The nation's earliest written literature, in Sanskrit, dates from the Lichhavi period (about A.D. 400 to 600). From this period through the 1700s, Nepal's written literature appeared in Sanskrit, Newari (a local language), and Nepali. These documents were religious texts, chronicles, property records, and so on. Most of this material is more historical than literary.

SPEAKING NEPALI

Learn a few simple phrases in Nepal's native language.

dhanyabaad (DAHN-yuh-bahd):
   thank you

namaste (nah-mu-STEH):
   hello, good-bye

sanchai (sun-SHY):
   how are you?

Literary writing in the Nepali language developed in the 1800s. About 1830 a group of Nepali poets began writing on themes from Hindu epics. In 1835 poet Bhanubhakta Acharya began translating the Hindu epic poem *Ramayana* into Nepali. This translation, published in 1887, became very popular for its conversational flavor, its religious sincerity, and its realistic natural descriptions.

One common theme among Himalayan legends—including Nepali folklore—is the yeti, or abominable snowman. The yeti resembles a huge man covered with shaggy fur. He is believed to live in the Himalayas near the snow line.

Modern Nepali literature began in the 1920s and 1930s with a group of writers who discarded the Sanskrit literary tradition. Instead, they adopted some Western literary forms, such as prose (nonrhyming) poetry, tragic drama, and the short story. Their work addressed the themes of love and patriotism as well as the problems of injustice, tyranny, and poverty.

Contemporary writers in Nepal usually favor Nepali and English over Sanskrit. Authors who use Sanskrit tend to imitate traditional styles, but others experiment with new forms. Many young writers address nationalist themes.

The government's ongoing effort to promote education and to increase literacy is strongly—and positively—affecting Nepal's literary scene. This effort is producing more and more Nepalis who are able and inspired to write. It also encourages authors to write more. As a result, Nepali literature is growing faster than ever.

Music

Hinduism teaches that music and dance come directly from the gods. A Hindu legend says that the god Brahma sang the Vedas, repeating them continuously. The storm god Rudra, an incarnation of Shiva, is also closely connected with song and dance. The *rudra-vina*, a zither-like stringed instrument, takes its name from this god. With such roots, many Nepalis view music and dance as more than just entertainment. To sing, to dance, or to play an instrument is to worship.

Classical Nepali music, like the classical music of Pakistan, Bangladesh, and northern India, is based on ragas. Ragas are melodic patterns upon which musicians and singers compose and improvise. After a musician chooses a raga, he or she explores its infinite variations, often creating a hypnotic effect on listeners. Different ragas represent different moods, gods, times of day, or seasons.

Nepali folk music uses mostly wind, string, and percussion

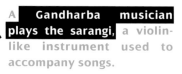

A **Gandharba musician plays the sarangi,** a violin-like instrument used to accompany songs.

instruments. This music strongly resembles folk music from the world's other mountainous regions, such as old-time Appalachian music of North America. Nepal's official folk music ambassadors are the Gandharbas. The Gandharbas are the only Nepali musician caste. Their rank is very low. But in Hindu mythology, they were once the winged musicians of the gods. For centuries they traveled from village to village playing music, spreading news, and preserving folklore. Listeners paid them with small amounts of food and money. Modern media are quickly taking over the Gandharbas' role, making their difficult lives even harder.

Like many other countries, Nepal feels the influence of Western music. Nepal's rock music scene began in the 1960s and 1970s, when thousands of counterculture youth from Europe and North America flocked to Kathmandu—especially a street named Jochhen Tole (better known as Freak Street). During this time, Nepal's own rock pioneers emerged. Throughout the following decades, Nepali popular music expanded to include many of the styles common around the world. As in any country, Nepal's popular music blends old and native influences with new and imported ones.

Food

Most Nepalis have diets based heavily on grains. In the Terai, rice is the staple food. Corn and the grain millet are more widely available in the Hills. In the Himalayas, the potato is the staple food.

Nepalis also eat many seasonal vegetables and fruits. For example, pumpkins, green peppers, onions, cucumbers, apples, apricots, and plums are common. The Nepali diet includes a wide range of legumes (beans and peas) as well, often served in the form of dal (lentil soup). A typical Nepali meal consists of dal, *bhat* (steamed rice), and *tarkari* (vegetables), also known as "the trinity." People eat poultry, fish, eggs, and meat (lamb, goat, buffalo, and yak) infrequently and in small quantities.

A bowl of dal *(right)* accompanies a **typical Nepali meal** of rice, vegetables, and fried egg.

The country's most popular beverage is *chiya*—also known as chai—which is strong black tea brewed with milk, sugar, and spices. Another popular Nepali brew is chyaang, a beer made from fermented barley, corn, rye, or millet.

Nepali food is very spicy. Curries (blends of spices), chilies, and ginger season the otherwise simple dishes. Food choices are closely linked with Nepal's numerous holidays and festivals. On special occasions, people indulge in more expensive foods, such as sweets made with molasses, sesame seeds, and nuts.

NEPALI CHIYA (CHAI)

1 cup milk

1 tea bag or 1 tablespoon black tea, Nepali or Indian

1 teaspoon sugar

⅛ teaspoon ground cardamom

Pour milk into a small saucepan. Stir in the other ingredients. Over low heat, bring the mixture to a boil. Let it simmer for about 5 minutes. Pour into a cup (or through a tea strainer if using loose tea). Serve hot. Makes one serving.

Newar sculptures and carvings cover this pagoda-style Hindu temple in the ancient village of Panauti, part of modern Kathmandu.

⊙ Art and Architecture

Nepal has a rich artistic heritage that draws from Indian, Tibetan, Hindu, and Buddhist traditions, as well as from local influences. The history of Nepal's art and architecture stretches over more than two thousand years.

During two periods in Nepal's past—the seventh century and the eleventh to fourteenth centuries—Nepali culture experienced artistic surges. People throughout southern and eastern Asia admired and imitated Nepali sculpture, painting, and architecture during these periods.

In the late thirteenth century, Tibet invited Newar artists and architects to travel north and share their skills. These masters introduced the pagoda and other Newar styles to eastern Asia. Eventually Tibetan motifs likewise found their way into Nepali art. Chinese and Tibetan symbols, such as the dragon and the phoenix (a mythical bird), began to appear among Newar symbols.

The Newar became such skilled artisans that they are almost entirely responsible for Nepali contributions to world culture. Most of Nepal's famous religious structures are in the Kathmandu Valley, the home of the Newar people. In addition to architecture, the Newar excel in wood carving, metalworking, and painting.

Although artistic expression suffered strict censorship during the one hundred years of Rana rule, it has revived since the 1950s. Modern Nepali visual art mostly falls into two distinct categories: traditional idealistic paintings and Western-style works. Modern Nepali art is known for its natural, Tantric, and social themes.

Sports and Recreation

Most Nepalis are poor and work long days. They therefore have little money or time for leisure activities. The most common forms of entertainment and recreation in Nepal are listening to folk music and attending community gatherings such as festivals and dances. Movies are popular in the cities and towns.

Many Nepali adults believe that games and sports are for children. Despite this attitude, the government strongly supports athletics. It registers forty-four official sports organizations. Popular sports in Nepal are soccer, cricket (a bat-and-ball game from Britain), basketball, table tennis, volleyball, badminton, and a southern Asian game called *kabaddi*.

The game of kabaddi originated in India about four thousand years ago. It developed as a way to hone self-defense techniques. It combines characteristics of wrestling and rugby, requiring both skill and strength.

Nepal is a prime destination for outdoor enthusiasts from around the world. Its churning rivers thrill whitewater rafters. Its relatively pristine countryside lures hikers. And its

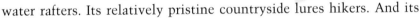

People come from around the world to play **elephant polo in Nepal.** Players riding the elephants use a long-handled mallet to hit a ball into a goal.

mountains, home to many of the world's highest peaks, attract ambitious climbers.

Holidays and Festivals

Nepal may be poor in some ways, but it is rich in celebration. Nepalis observe at least three dozen major holidays. Most festivals follow a lunar calendar, so their dates shift from year to year. Some of Nepal's most important festivals are Nava Barsha, Baisakh Purnima, Teej, Dashain, and Tihar.

Nava Barsha is Nepal's New Year's Day. It usually falls in the second week of April. Nepalis celebrate this national holiday by getting together with family and friends, picnicking, and socializing in various ways.

In April or May, Nepalis celebrate Baisakh Purnima, a triple anniversary of Buddhism. This festival honors the day Buddha was born, the day he was enlightened, and the day he entered nirvana. On this national holiday, people revere Buddha at Nepal's holiest Buddhist sites, such as Swayambhunath temple, Bodhnath stupa, and Buddha's birthplace in Lumbini.

In August or September, Nepali women celebrate the Hindu festival of Teej. Mothers send gifts of food and clothing to their grown daughters' houses. Groups of women clad in red (a Hindu bridal color) gather to feast, sing folk songs, and dance. The women then fast and pray for happy marriages and healthy families.

> Visit www.vgsbooks.com for links to websites with additional information about Nepal's culture. Listen to samples of Nepali music, view pictures of pagodas, and try out different recipes for Nepali food.

Boys compare spools of string for kite flying at the **Dashain festival.**

Dashain, celebrated for two weeks in September or October, is Nepal's most important festival. It celebrates the inevitable triumph of good over evil. Dashain is a time for exchanging gifts and blessings, gathering with family, feasting, kite flying, and performing rituals to honor Durga, the Hindu goddess of victory.

Nepalis celebrate Tihar, the Hindu festival of lights, in October or November. Tihar is Nepal's second most important holiday. In honor of Lakshmi, the goddess of wealth, every home and building displays rows of lights.

THE ECONOMY

Nepal's high mountains and isolated valleys make transportation, communication, and construction difficult. As a result, the nation's rugged terrain has hampered economic development. One hundred years of Rana policies also held the country back. When the Shah monarchy returned to power in the 1950s, Nepal began to develop schools, hospitals, roads, telecommunications, electric power, and industry. But it had a lot of catching up to do.

Although the government has laid the foundation for economic growth, Nepal remains one of the poorest and least developed countries in the world. Its average annual income per person is only about $290—a figure that ranks among the twelve lowest in the world. About 40 percent of Nepalis live in extreme poverty. Political instability and civil war in the 1990s and 2000s have stifled Nepal's economy. Inefficiency, weak oversight, outdated technology, geographic isolation, and natural disasters have posed other obstacles. Development has barely kept pace with Nepal's growing population.

Experts expect the population to continue increasing and straining the nation's resources.

○ Services

Nepal's service sector includes commerce, transportation, telecommunications, hotels, bars, restaurants, financial services, housing, and government services. This sector is responsible for 42 percent of the nation's gross domestic product (GDP). The GDP is the total value of goods and services produced inside the country each year. Service jobs employ 18 percent of the nation's labor force.

Nepal's service sector is somewhat lopsided. Nepali transportation, communication, finance, and social welfare services are growing compared to Nepal's overall economic development. However, their growth is slow. And public utility services, such as electricity, gas, and drinking water, are growing even more slowly. They are currently limited to urban and tourist areas. Nepal's service sector depends

ECOTOURISM

Tourism has done wonders for the Nepali economy, and it promises to continue growing. But tourism is a double-edged sword. As more and more foreigners visit Nepal, they stress its fragile environment. Eventually, if developers and visitors damage the nation's flora, fauna, land, air, and water too much, tourists will no longer want to visit.

To earn tourism income without destroying its natural resources, Nepal is trying to develop more ecotourism. International media coverage has made tourists more aware of the environmental damage they can cause. Some hotels and resorts attract concerned tourists by developing environmentally safe structures and activities. Lower environmental impact leads to better tourist satisfaction, which in turn leads to repeat visits and word-of-mouth promotion. This helps local communities by spurring business growth and reducing poverty.

Tourists go on an **elephant safari in Chitwan National Park.** Critics argue that safari companies abuse elephants and damage parkland.

heavily on tourism, which provides opportunities for retail businesses, hotels, and restaurants.

Because Rana rulers followed a strict policy of isolation from 1846 to 1951, Nepal didn't begin to develop a tourist industry until the Shah monarchy returned to power. Since then tourism has expanded rapidly. In 1962 only about 6,000 tourists visited Nepal. In 2005 more than 375,000 tourists visited. Money spent by foreigners in Nepal has helped improve the country's economic situation. Tourism brings in about $150 million per year. It offers Nepal great potential for economic growth.

Agriculture

Nepal's agricultural sector includes farming, forestry, and fishing. This sector is responsible for 38 percent of the nation's GDP. It employs 76 percent of the nation's labor force.

Although the vast majority of Nepalis depend on farming for survival, only about 20 percent of the country's land can be cultivated. One-third of this fertile area lies in the Hills. Most of the remaining two-thirds of farmable land is in the Terai.

Almost all Nepal's farms are small family plots worked with traditional hand tools. Only a few large farms in the Terai use modern machinery. Most Nepalis survive by growing barely enough grain and vegetables for their own households. In many areas, the land provides food for only half the year. Young men often work for long periods in India and send cash home to support their families.

Farmers throughout Nepal grow corn, wheat, and millet. Terai farmers also grow rice, and mountain farmers grow

Because Nepal is land-locked, it has no large-scale fishing industry. However, the government has actively developed aquaculture (fish farming) as one way to relieve malnutrition and rural poverty.

A farmer in the Terai uses yoked oxen to pull a wood-and-steel plow through his fields. Many small farms in Nepal use such low-cost methods.

potatoes. In addition, many farmers raise goats, buffalo, yaks, and sheep for wool, milk, and meat—or as work animals. Nepal is home to some tea plantations and fruit orchards. In the Terai, large farms grow sugarcane and jute (a plant used to make rope) for export. In good years, Nepal can also export rice and potatoes. In bad years, the nation must import grains to feed its people.

To open up farmland and obtain fuel and building materials, poor Nepalis have historically cut down trees. Nepal was once rich in timber, but only 29 percent of its land remains forested. Nonetheless, timber is still a key resource. Most locals still use wood for everyday fuel and housing needs. Some harvest timber for profit. Nepal's forests also provide homes for hundreds of animal species. This rich biodiversity is important to Nepal's environmental and economic health. To protect its forest resources while addressing the needs of rural Nepalis, the government has established a nationwide program of community-based forest management.

CHILD LABOR

Poor families in Nepal often have no choice but to send their children to work instead of school. Lack of education keeps the poverty cycle spinning into the next generation. Experts estimate that about 25 percent of Nepali children between four and five years old are engaged in some kind of family or wage labor.

◉ Industry

Nepal's industrial sector includes energy, manufacturing, and mining. This sector is responsible for 20 percent of the nation's GDP. It employs 6 percent of the nation's labor force.

A boy makes pots for his family's pottery business in Bhaktapur.

Workers sort stones for building material near a brick kiln in Kathmandu.

Nepal's energy resources are limited. It has small fossil fuel deposits but doesn't extract these fuels. Biofuels (wood and animal dung) provide 87 percent of the energy Nepalis use. Imported fossil fuels and domestic hydropower provide the rest. Scientists estimate that Nepal uses less than 1 percent of its feasible hydropower. They say that if Nepal were to harness its full waterpower potential, it could meet all its energy needs. It could also sell electricity to neighboring countries.

Because biofuels and fossil fuels often harm the environment and human health, many Nepalis are developing other energy sources. These sources are not only cleaner but also cheaper and easier to obtain. The government of Nepal, the United Nations, and many other organizations are helping Nepalis develop such sources—and tools that use them. These sources and tools are called rural energy technologies. They include biogas (dung converted into natural gas), gasifiers (machines that turn wood, dung, or coal into cleaner-burning gas), water mills, small-scale hydroelectric dams, wind power, solar power, and many household tools powered by solar cells.

Most of Nepal's manufacturing uses the nation's natural resources and farm products or depends on materials imported from India. Jute plants and clothing factories were among Nepal's first industries. They emerged in the 1940s, when high prices in India prompted both Indians and Nepalis to open plants in the Terai, where production costs were lower. Later manufacturing development has depended largely on foreign aid.

A **Gurung woman spins wool for yarn** in the village of Muktinath. Many Gurung people living in the mountains survive through cottage industries such as raising sheep for wool and meat.

Nepal's modern manufacturing focuses on food (sugar, beer, cigarettes, and vegetable oils); textiles (jute and shoes); wood (paper, matches, and lumber); and construction materials (cement, bricks, and tiles). Traditional cottage industries (small family businesses) are also important. Cottage industries produce carpets, baskets, furniture, and soap.

Nepali manufacturing has grown very slowly because start-up money, expertise, and energy supplies are chronically scarce. Poorly developed markets, inadequate transportation, and competition from cheap imported goods also pose challenges.

In the past, Nepal mined several metals: gold, copper, lead, nickel, iron, and cobalt. All these activities except gold mining have declined. Scientists believe that Nepal may have a lot of undiscovered gold, lead, and zinc. Its future metal mining is likely to focus on these three resources.

Nepal's nonmetal mineral resources include limestone, marble, dolomite, talc, magnesite, granite, syenite, slate, boulder, gravel, sand, and clay. Mining for these minerals—especially those useful in construction—is active. The country also has gem-quality and industrial-grade ruby, sapphire, aquamarine, tourmaline, and quartz deposits. These resources are mostly untapped.

Foreign Trade

Nepal's most important trading partner is India, for both geographical and historical reasons. Nepal has tried to expand its foreign trade via agreements with other nations, such as China, Pakistan, Bangladesh, the United States, the United Kingdom, Singapore, Thailand, Germany, and Japan. But India still dominates this aspect of Nepal's economy, accounting for nearly 65 percent of foreign trade. Other nations supply the remaining 35 percent of foreign trade.

Nepal imports far more goods than it exports. Imports (mainly petroleum products, fertilizer, and machinery) are responsible for about 75 percent of Nepal's foreign trade. Exports (clothing, carpets, grain, and leather) account for about 25 percent of foreign trade.

Transportation

Nepal's transportation system is relatively underdeveloped. Poor infrastructure (public works such as roads) has hindered the nation's economy. But Nepal is using foreign aid to gradually improve the quality and number of its roads, airports, and railways.

Nepal's network of roads is sparse and unreliable. It has about 10,942 miles (17,609 km) of roads. About 30 percent of these roads are paved, 27 percent are gravel, and 43 percent are dirt. A few major

A bus pauses at a river crossing near the town of Besisahar. Nepal's rugged terrain makes road building and maintenance difficult.

Nepal has no rail system, but the government operates a short railway in the Terai. It links Jaynagar, India, with Janakpur, Nepal. These cities are only 18 miles (29 km) apart, but no road connects them. The railway's rickety old train sees heavy use because Janakpur is home to an important temple.

highways connect large cities and stretch to the borders. But the main means of travel in Nepal is the web of trails and footpaths crisscrossing the mountains and valleys.

Aviation plays a vital role in linking Nepali communities, especially in the hills and mountains, where roads are poor and scarce. Several airlines provide service among Nepal's cities and towns. Most of Nepal's fifty regional airports are grassy fields without modern navigation systems. Tribhuvan International Airport outside Kathmandu is Nepal's central—and most modern—airport. It provides international flights to thirty-five countries.

Communications

Like Nepal's transportation, the country's communication services are limited. Many Nepalis can't access the postal service. Few households own telephones, although urban areas offer public telephone service. Most private homes don't have computers or Internet access either. However, both are available to city dwellers via Internet cafés.

Nepal's constitution guarantees freedom of the press. For those who can afford radios and televisions, Radio Nepal and Nepal Television broadcast news, music, and other programming in Nepali and English. In remote areas, foreign television programs are available via satellite. Nepal's major newspapers include *Gorkhapatra*, *Kantipur*, and The *Himalayan Times*.

The Future

Nepal faces many pressing economic and social challenges. To reduce poverty and improve the well-being of its growing population, Nepal must strengthen and expand virtually every sector of its economy, administration, and infrastructure.

To meet these challenges, Nepal needs money—and lots of it. Tourism and hydroelectricity offer great income potential for Nepal. These two endeavors may help the nation become financially self-sufficient. But before Nepal can tap this potential, it requires something even more basic: peace.

Members of Nepal's Maoist Party celebrate their party's success in the 2008 elections. The Maoists received the most votes of any party in the election.

Nepal is an ancient land with many centuries of struggle behind it. Even so, the late twentieth and early twenty-first centuries have proven to be some of Nepal's most difficult years. Several decades of political instability followed by a decade-long civil war made the already hard lives of Nepalis nearly unbearable.

That dark period, Nepalis believe, has finally passed. With its civil war over and a new government freely and fairly elected in 2008, Nepal has high hopes for a brighter, more prosperous future.

Visit www.vgsbooks.com for links to websites with additional information about Nepal's economy and development. Learn about Nepal's current efforts to improve roads and other infrastructure.

CA. 60,000,000 B.C. The shifting Indian subcontinent crashes into the fixed Asian continent. The Himalayas begin to emerge.

CA. 3500 B.C. People living in the Kathmandu Valley leave behind tools made of polished stone.

1600s-1400s B.C. The Gopala tribe settles the Kathmandu Valley.

1400s-1300s B.C. The Abhiras conquer the Gopalas.

1300s B.C. The Kiratas conquer the Abhiras.

1000 B.C. Written references to the people and land of Nepal appear.

563 B.C. Siddhartha Gautama (Buddha) is born in Lumbini.

A.D. 100 The oldest known epigraph in Nepal is created. The Lichhavi dynasty begins ruling the Kathmandu Valley.

464-505 King Manadeva I erects an inscribed pillar—Nepal's oldest important written record—at the Changu Narayan temple.

600s The city of Lalitpur is founded.

602 The Thakuri dynasty begins ruling the Kathmandu Valley.

800s-1100s Internal conflict, foreign invasions, and natural disasters constantly disrupt society during Nepal's dark age.

LATE 900s King Gunakamadeva founds the city of Kantipur.

CA. 1200 The Malla dynasty begins ruling the Kathmandu Valley.

1300s Nepalis begin collecting oral history in written chronicles.

1400s-1500s The Mughal dynasty conquers much of India. Indian princes flee and establish small kingdoms, including Gurkha, in central and western Nepal.

1500-1700s The Shah dynasty gradually expands Gurkha territory to include all of modern Nepal.

1559 The Shah dynasty begins with Dravya Shah, ruler of Gurkha.

1769 Prithvi Narayan Shah establishes the Kingdom of Nepal.

LATE 1700s Nepal expands to twice its modern size. Nepal and Tibet battle over trade issues.

1814-1816 Nepal and Great Britain fight the Anglo-Nepali War. Nepal loses, and the Treaty of Segauli dramatically shrinks Nepali territory.

EARLY 1800s Weak Shah kings make the post of prime minister very powerful. Nepali literature is born.

1846 Prime Minister Jung Bahadur takes over Nepal and adds Rana to his name. A century of Rana rule begins.

1850 Jung Bahadur establishes isolationist policies.

1857-1858 Gurkha soldiers fight in the British Army during the Indian Rebellion. In return, Great Britain restores much of Nepal's territory. Nepal assumes its modern shape and size.

1930s-1940s Opposition to Rana rule grows throughout Nepal.

1950 Anti-Rana factions join forces. Public rebellion erupts.

1951 Rana rule ends. King Tribhuvan Shah retakes the throne.

1959 King Mahendra Shah enacts Nepal's first constitution.

1962 Mahendra enacts a new constitution, establishing a partyless panchayat system that guarantees his ultimate authority.

1960s-1970s European and North American youths flock to Kathmandu.

1970s Students demonstrate against the panchayat system and for human rights.

1980 King Birendra Shah orders a national referendum on the panchayat system. Nepalis choose to keep the panchayat system.

1980s Infighting weakens both the panchayat system and the opposition movement.

1990 Birendra scraps the panchayat system and begins working with his opponents. Nepal becomes a parliamentary democracy under a constitutional monarch.

1990s A series of unstable governments rule Nepal. Communism gains popularity. A Maoist insurgency is born.

1996 The Nepali Civil War begins between Maoists and the government.

2001 Prince Dipendra kills several members of the royal family, including himself and his father. Birendra's brother Gyanendra becomes king.

2005 King Gyanendra seizes full control of Nepal. In response, the Maoists join forces with mainstream political parties to reduce his power.

2006 The Nepali Civil War ends. A peace agreement creates an interim constitution and schedules elections for a new Constituent Assembly.

2007 Sporadic violence and political disagreements delay elections.

2008 Maoists win the most seats in April elections. All parties agree to end the monarchy.

COUNTRY NAME Nepal

AREA 56,827 square miles (147,181 sq. km)

MAIN LANDFORMS Terai, Siwalik Range, Mahabharat Range, the Hills region, Kathmandu Valley, Greater Himalayas

HIGHEST POINT Mount Everest, 29,035 feet (8,850 m) above sea level

LOWEST POINT Kanchan Kalan, 230 feet (70 m) above sea level

MAJOR RIVERS Karnali River, Narayani River, Kosi River

ANIMALS black bears, crocodiles, elephants, foxes, Gangetic dolphins, king cobras, leopards, musk deer, rhinoceroses, snow cocks, snow leopards, snow partridges, tigers, wild boars, wild goats and sheep, wildcats, yaks

CAPITAL CITY Kathmandu

OTHER MAJOR CITIES Biratnagar, Lalitpur, Pokhara

OFFICIAL LANGUAGE Nepali

MONETARY UNIT Nepali rupee. 100 paisa = 1 rupee.

CURRENCY

Nepal's currency is the Nepali rupee. Its international currency code is NPR, and its written symbol is Rs. The government introduced the rupee in 1932 to replace the mohar currency in circulation at the time. Coins come in denominations of 1, 5, 10, 25, and 50 paisa and 1, 2, 5, and 10 rupees. Paper notes come in denominations of 1, 2, 5, 10, 20, 50, 100, 500, and 1,000 rupees.

Nepal adopted its current flag on December 12, 1962. It is the only nonrectangular national flag in the world. Its double-triangle shape developed in the late 1800s, when Nepal combined the pennants (triangular flags) of the Shah and Rana families into a single flag. The moon in the top part represented the Shah family of kings. The sun in the bottom part symbolized the Rana family of prime ministers. Modern Nepalis say the images portray their hope that Nepal will last as long as the sun and moon. The flag's background color, crimson, is Nepal's national color.

"Sayaun Thunga Phool Ka" (Hundreds of Flowers) is Nepal's national anthem. When the Nepali Civil War ended in 2006, the government wanted to replace its pro-monarchy anthem. It held a public contest and received more than twelve hundred submissions. Poet Pradeep Kumar Rai (writing under the pen name Byakul Maila) won the contest. Ambar Gurung wrote the melody. Nepal officially announced its new anthem on August 3, 2007. The entire Nepali anthem, translated into English, appears below.

Hundreds of Flowers

We are hundreds of flowers, the one garland—Nepali
Sovereign, spread out from Mechi to Mahakali.

Amassing nature's millions of resources
By the blood of heroes, independent and immovable.

Land of knowledge, land of peace, Terai hills, mountains
Indivisible this beloved, our motherland Nepal.

The diverse races, languages, faiths, and cultures are so extensive
Our progressive nation, long live Nepal.

To see the musical notation and hear the melody and Nepali lyrics of the nation's national anthem, visit www.vgsbooks.com.

BHANUBHAKTA ACHARYA (1814–1868) Bhanubhakta Acharya was the first Nepali writer to create a major work in the Nepali language. He was born in Chundi Ramgha in central Nepal. His father was a government official in western Nepal. His grandfather educated him at home. In 1835 Bhanubhakta began translating the Hindu epic poem *Ramayana* from Sanskrit into Nepali. This translation, published in 1887 after his death, became very popular for its conversational flavor, religious sincerity, and realistic natural descriptions.

ARNIKO (ca. 1244–1305) Arniko was one of the greatest architects of all Asia. He was born in Lalitpur, and his parents named him Balabahu. In 1260 China's emperor, Kublai Khan, asked Nepal to send an architect to Tibet to supervise construction of a Buddhist shrine there. Nepal's king chose the teenage Balabahu over eighty others. He went on to design and build many famous structures in China and became known throughout Asia by the Chinese name Arniko. Historians credit him with spreading the pagoda architectural style.

JUNG BAHADUR (1817–1877) Jung Bahadur was prime minister of Nepal from 1846 to 1877. He founded the powerful Rana dynasty of prime ministers, which ruled until 1951. He was born Bir Narsingh Kunwar, but he became famous as Jung Bahadur, a name his uncle gave him. He added the honorific Rana to his name after seizing power. Though he began a dynasty that developed into a dictatorship, he also made some positive contributions to Nepali history. His rule improved foreign relations, made sweeping legal reforms, and preserved Nepal's independence while nearly all its neighbors became European colonies.

PUSHPA KAMAL DAHAL (b. 1954) Pushpa Kamal Dahal is the leader of Nepal's Maoists. He was born to a peasant family in northwestern Nepal. His family moved to the Terai, where their fortunes improved. He became a Communist in high school and later earned a bachelor's degree in agriculture. He rose to lead Nepal's Communist Party in 1986. He is better known by his war name Prachanda, which means "the fierce one." After the Maoist victory in Nepal's April 2008 elections, Prachanda expected to become the nation's new leader.

SIDDHARTHA GAUTAMA (ca. 563–483 B.C.) Siddhartha Gautama founded Buddhism. He was born a Hindu prince at Lumbini in central Nepal. At twenty-nine, he left his palace for the first time and saw people suffering. Disturbed by these sights, he gave up worldly life and meditated for six years. This experience led him to enlightenment, and he became known as Buddha. He began traveling around the region and teaching that desire causes suffering and that eliminating desire can end sorrow.

JHAMAK GHIMIRE (b. 1980) Jhamak Ghimire is a Nepali writer. She has severe cerebral palsy and cannot walk, sit upright, or use her arms. As a child, she taught herself to read and to write with her toes. She burst onto

Nepal's literary scene at the age of nineteen. Since then she has published several books of poetry, songs, journal entries, stories, and essays; has won multiple literary awards; and has become a columnist for the newspaper *Kantipur*. Her journey has earned her the nickname the Helen Keller of Nepal. She lives with her family in Kachide in eastern Nepal.

NARAYAN GOPAL (1939–1990) Narayan Gopal was a performer and composer of modern Nepali music. He was born to a Newar family in Kathmandu. His father was a classical musician and wanted his son to be one too. Gopal showed musical talent at an early age, but he preferred modern styles. He studied music in India and went on to record more than five hundred songs. His recordings—mostly love songs—have remained popular long after his death. Nepali radio stations continue to play them every day. Nepalis call him King of Singers.

PASANG LLAMU (1961–1993) Pasang Llamu was the first Nepali woman to reach the summit of Mount Everest. She was born to a Sherpa family in northeastern Nepal, the only girl of five children. She grew up in a society that trapped women at home and told them they could never stand atop Everest. When Llamu reached the summit in April 1993, she shattered cultural barriers for Nepali women. She died on her descent. More than twenty thousand people followed her funeral procession. Nepalis continue to honor Llamu as a national hero.

TENZING NORGAY (1914–1986) Tenzing Norgay and Edmund Hillary were the first people known to have reached the summit of Mount Everest. Norgay grew up in a Sherpa family in northeastern Nepal. He began mountaineering in the 1930s. He reached the summit of Everest with Hillary in 1953 and subsequently became an international hero. He continued climbing—and training other climbers—after Everest. He died in Darjeeling, India, of cerebral bleeding.

BIRENDRA SHAH (1945–2001) Birendra Shah was king of Nepal from 1972 to 2001. He was born in Kathmandu and spent much of his youth studying abroad. When he became king, he continued his father's absolute monarchy. In the 1980s and 1990s, he grew more open to democracy. His willingness to adapt earned him high esteem from most Nepalis. He died in 2001 after being shot by his son Dipendra.

PRITHVI NARAYAN SHAH (1723–1775) Prithvi Narayan Shah was the first ruler of the modern Kingdom of Nepal. Born in Gurcha, he was a descendant of Dravya Shah, who founded the Shah dynasty of Gurkha. He became the king of Gurkha in 1743. By 1769 he controlled about one-third of modern Nepal, including the Kathmandu Valley. He called his new realm—which included parts of the Terai, the hills, and the Himalayas—the Kingdom of Nepal. This realm laid the social, geographic, and political foundation for modern Nepal.

Sights to See

The U.S. Department of State has issued a travel warning (http:// travel.state.gov/travel/cis_pa_tw/tw/tw_927.html) for Nepal because conditions in the country may become dangerous.

BODHNATH STUPA Bodhnath stupa, a huge dome-shaped Buddhist shrine on the outskirts of Kathmandu, is the center of Tibetan Buddhism in Nepal. At 118 feet (36 m) tall, it is one of the largest stupas in southern Asia. Bodhnath has been a sacred site since the A.D. 600s, but the present stupa dates from the 1300s. It reportedly entombs a wise man revered by both Buddhists and Hindus. Pilgrims walk clockwise around the stupa while spinning the prayer wheels set into its base.

CHITWAN NATIONAL PARK Chitwan National Park, established in 1973, was Nepal's first national park. It protects 360 square miles (932 sq. km) of tropical forest—one of the few undisturbed remnants of the Terai. It is home to hundreds of animal species but is particularly famous for its endangered animals, such as the one-horned Indian rhinoceros, the Bengal tiger, the gharial crocodile, and the Gangetic dolphin.

EVEREST (SAGARMATHA) NATIONAL PARK Sagarmatha National Park protects 443 square miles (1,148 sq. km) of the Greater Himalayas. It contains Mount Everest and several other of the world's highest peaks. Locally known as the Khumbu region, it is the homeland of Nepal's Sherpa people.

KATHMANDU DURBAR SQUARE Durbar Square is the ancient heart of Kathmandu. It is a complex of buildings founded during the Lichhavi dynasty (A.D. 100s–600s). Until the late 1700s, it served as the Nepali royal family's residence. The complex is divided into two main courtyards. Around these are scattered some of Kathmandu's finest temples and other historic buildings, including the city's namesake, Kasthamandap.

LUMBINI Lumbini is the birthplace of Siddharth Gautama (Buddha). Located in the western Terai, it is one of four main pilgrimage sites for all Buddhists. The site contains a temple marking the exact birthplace of Buddha, a pillar built by the Indian emperor Asoka, ruins of ancient monasteries, and many other religious structures.

PASHUPATINATH Pashupatinath, a temple devoted to the Hindu god Shiva, is Nepal's holiest Hindu site. It lies on the Bagmati River in the eastern outskirts of Kathmandu. Pilgrims from all over Nepal come here to worship, bathe, and spend their last days. On the banks of the river are raised platforms used as cremation sites. Only Hindus are allowed inside the temple complex, but non-Hindu visitors may view it from across the river.

animism: a system of belief in spirits that inhabit natural places, beings, things, and the everyday world, and that influence human lives and fortunes

castes: hereditary social classes. Castes form a ladder of religious and social rank among Hindus. Occupation, family status, and other social criteria determine an individual's assignment to one of dozens of castes.

colonial: controlled by a foreign power

Communism: a political and economic theory supporting community ownership of all property. Its goal is to create equality.

constitution: a document defining the basic principles and laws of a nation

deforestation: the loss of forests due to logging or clearing land for human uses. Deforestation leads to soil erosion, loss of wildlife habitat, and global warming.

democracy: government by the people through free elections

gross domestic product (GDP): the total value of goods and services produced inside a country over a period of time, usually one year

hydroelectric power: electricity produced by damming a river and then harnessing the energy of rushing water at hydroelectric power stations

literacy: the ability to read, write, and do basic math

Maoists: people who follow the Communist ideas of China's Mao Zedong, which focus on the importance of rural peasants

monarchy: government by a hereditary leader who has a lifetime term

monsoon: seasonal wind reversal

panchayat system: system of government in Nepal from 1962 to 1990, based on elected village councils

plantations: large farms producing cash crops such as timber or tea

Glossary

Selected Bibliography

Central Bureau of Statistics. August 17, 2007.
http://www.cbs.gov.np (April 28, 2008).
This Nepali government website is an excellent source of facts and figures on many social and economic topics, such as population, agriculture, manufacturing, living standards, and labor.

Digital Himalaya. March 28, 2008.
http://www.digitalhimalaya.com (April 28, 2008).
The mission of this website is to preserve and provide public access to Himalayan artifacts that are decaying in their original forms. The collection includes films, photos, recordings, maps, rare journals, and more. All are usable online.

Economic Survey: Fiscal Year 2006/2007. July 2007.
http://www.mof.gov.np/publication/budget/2007/surveyeng.php (April 28, 2008).
This Nepali government website offers access to the full text of its latest economic report. The report includes statistics and analysis on all aspects of Nepal's economy, including banking, foreign trade, poverty, employment, agriculture, industry, services, transportation, and communications.

FAO Country Profiles and Mapping Information System: Nepal. 2008.
http://www.fao.org/countryprofiles/index.asp?iso3=NPL&lang=en (April 28, 2008).
This website links readers to detailed articles and maps describing the environment, economy, agriculture, forestry, and fishing of Nepal.

Geology of Nepal. 2006.
http://www.ranjan.net.np/geologyofnepal.htm (April 28, 2008).
A professor of geology at Tribhuvan University maintains this website. In it he explains how the Himalayas formed and produced Nepal's unique geological and climatic zones.

Levy, Robert I. *Mesocosm: Hinduism and the Organization of a Traditional Newar City in Nepal.* Berkeley: University of California Press, 1990.
This book describes the development of Newar society in the city of Bhaktapur. By focusing on one of Nepal's most important cities—and the dominant ethnic group there—it offers a unique and close-up look at Nepali history, religion, and culture.

Nepal Journals Online. 2008.
http://www.nepjol.info (April 28, 2008).
This website provides free online access to journals publishing the research of Nepali scholars. Its two dozen journals discuss a variety of topics, from history to business to the sciences. Most articles are available in full text.

Nepal Population Report 2007. 2007.
http://www.moh.gov.np/population/publications.asp (April 28, 2008).
This Nepali government website offers access to the full text of its latest population report. The report includes statistics and analysis on fertility, mortality, aging, migration, urbanization, education, language, religion, ethnicity, health, status of women, employment, poverty, and more.

Parajulee, Ramjee. *The Democratic Transition in Nepal.* **Lanham, MD: Rowman & Littlefield Publishers, 2000.**
This book provides a very detailed and thorough study of the complex political and social developments in Nepal during the 1990s.

Plants of Nepal. **N.d.**
http://rbg-web2.rbge.org.uk/nepal (April 28, 2008).
This website, sponsored by the Royal Botanic Garden Edinburgh in Great Britain, offers a complete and reader-friendly guide to Nepal's climate and vegetation.

Population Reference Bureau. **April 24, 2008.**
http://www.prb.org (April 28, 2008).
The bureau offers current population figures, vital statistics, land area, and more. Special articles cover the latest environmental and health issues that concern each country.

Savada, Andrea Matles. *A Country Study: Nepal.* **Washington, DC: U.S. Government Printing Office, 1993.**
This is a comprehensive handbook on Nepal that gives background on the nation's geography, climate, history, economy, society, political affairs, and culture.

UN Nepal Information Platform. **April 28, 2008.**
http://www.un.org.np (April 28, 2008).
This website is the virtual home of the United Nations in Nepal. It offers links and information on Nepali humanitarian and development issues, including the latest election news.

Whelpton, John. *A History of Nepal.* **New York: Cambridge University Press, 2005.**
This book examines the economic, political, social, and cultural history of modern Nepal. It spans from the late eighteenth century to the early twenty-first century.

The World Factbook. **April 15, 2008.**
https://www.cia.gov/library/publications/the-world-factbook/geos/np.html (April 28, 2008).
This website features up-to-date information about the people, land, economy, and government of Nepal. It also briefly covers transnational issues.

Gunning for Nepal
http://www.time.com/time/asia/2005/nepal/story.html

This website provides an in-depth report on the Nepali Civil War published by *Time* magazine in April 2005. The site also provides links to interviews with King Gyanendra and Maoist leader Prachanda, as well as a photo essay on life as a Maoist rebel.

Majupuria, Indra. *Joys of Nepalese Cooking*. Gwalior, India: S. Devi, 1994.

This book presents 350 recipes from Nepal, providing a thorough treatment of Nepali cuisine. Each recipe gives step-by-step instructions, and many recipes feature drawings and photographs.

Mayhew, Bradley, Joe Bindloss, and Stan Armington. *Nepal*. Oakland: Lonely Planet Publications, 2006.

This travel guide provides in-depth information on Nepal's wide array of natural and historical landmarks, as well as on contemporary Nepali culture. The book also includes a summary of the country's history and politics.

Roberts-Davis, Tanya. *We Need to Go to School: Voices of the Rugmark Children*. Toronto: Groundwood Books, 2001.

In this young adult book, twenty former child carpet weavers in Nepal talk about their lives. They describe the harsh poverty that drove their families to send them to work, the virtual slave labor in the factories, and the hope they feel after being freed from their jobs and given the chance to attend school.

Spiny Babbler Museum
http://www.spinybabbler.org

This website is sponsored by a Kathmandu arts organization. The group formed in 1991 by publishing a journal of English poetry in Nepal. It grew into an art and literary gallery and began reaching out to underprivileged people all over Nepal. Its website offers a wealth of information on both modern and traditional Nepali visual arts, literature, music, and crafts.

Stewart, Whitney. *Sir Edmund Hillary: To Everest and Beyond*. Minneapolis: Twenty-First Century Books, 1996.

Edmund Hillary and Tenzing Norgay were the first people to stand on top of the tallest mountain in the world. This book describes how Hillary helped the Sherpas realize their dreams of a better life and searched for ways to balance environmental protection of the Himalayas with the economic benefits of tourism.

Tenzing, Tashi. *Tenzing Norgay and the Sherpas of Everest*. Camden, ME: Ragged Mountain Press, 2001.

In this book, Tenzing Norgay's grandson describes some of mountaineering's most famous climbs—focusing on Norgay himself, who made the first known summit of Mount Everest with Edmund Hillary in 1953. The author also discusses Sherpa history and society and explores the effects of mountaineering on Himalayan land and people.

Upadhyay, Samrat. *The Royal Ghosts.* **New York: Houghton Mifflin, 2006.**

This collection of short stories gives readers a peek at life in modern Kathmandu. It features characters trying to reconcile their dreams with the forces at work in Nepali society, such as civil war, duty to aging parents, the caste system, and arranged marriage.

vgsbooks.com
http://www.vgsbooks.com

Visit vgsbooks.com, the home page of the Visual Geography Series®. You can get linked to all sorts of useful online information, including geographical, historical, demographic, cultural, and economic websites. The vgsbooks.com site is a great resource for late-breaking news and statistics.

Wagle Street Journal
http://wagle.com.np/dinwag

This website is the personal blog of Dinesh Wagle, a young journalist for Nepal's newspaper *Kantipur*. His journal entries and commentary on current events offer an authentic view of real life in modern Nepal.

Welcome Nepal
http://www.welcomenepal.com

This is the official site of the Nepal Tourism Board. In addition to practical information for travelers, it describes the country's history, arts, culture, sports, geography, climate, and more.

Index

Captions for photos appearing on cover and chapter openers:

Cover: Annapurna, the tenth-highest mountain in the world, overlooks the Nepali village of Ghandrung.

pp. 4–5 Snow covers many Himalayan peaks throughout the year.

pp. 8–9 Terraced fields cover hillsides in the Terai region of southern Nepal.

pp. 36–37 Traditional and modern clothing styles mingle in a crowded Kathmandu market.

pp. 44–45 A child lights fireworks during the Tihar festival. Known as Diwali in India, this Hindu festival of lights takes place in late October or early November, the darkest time of the year.

pp. 56–57 Traders lead a string of pack horses across a suspension footbridge above the Kali Gandaki River in central Nepal.